# Happy Healthy Wealthy and Wise

# Happy Healthy Wealthy and Wise

## A daily companion guide for ordinary people who want extraordinary lives

Jill Wright

# CONTENTS

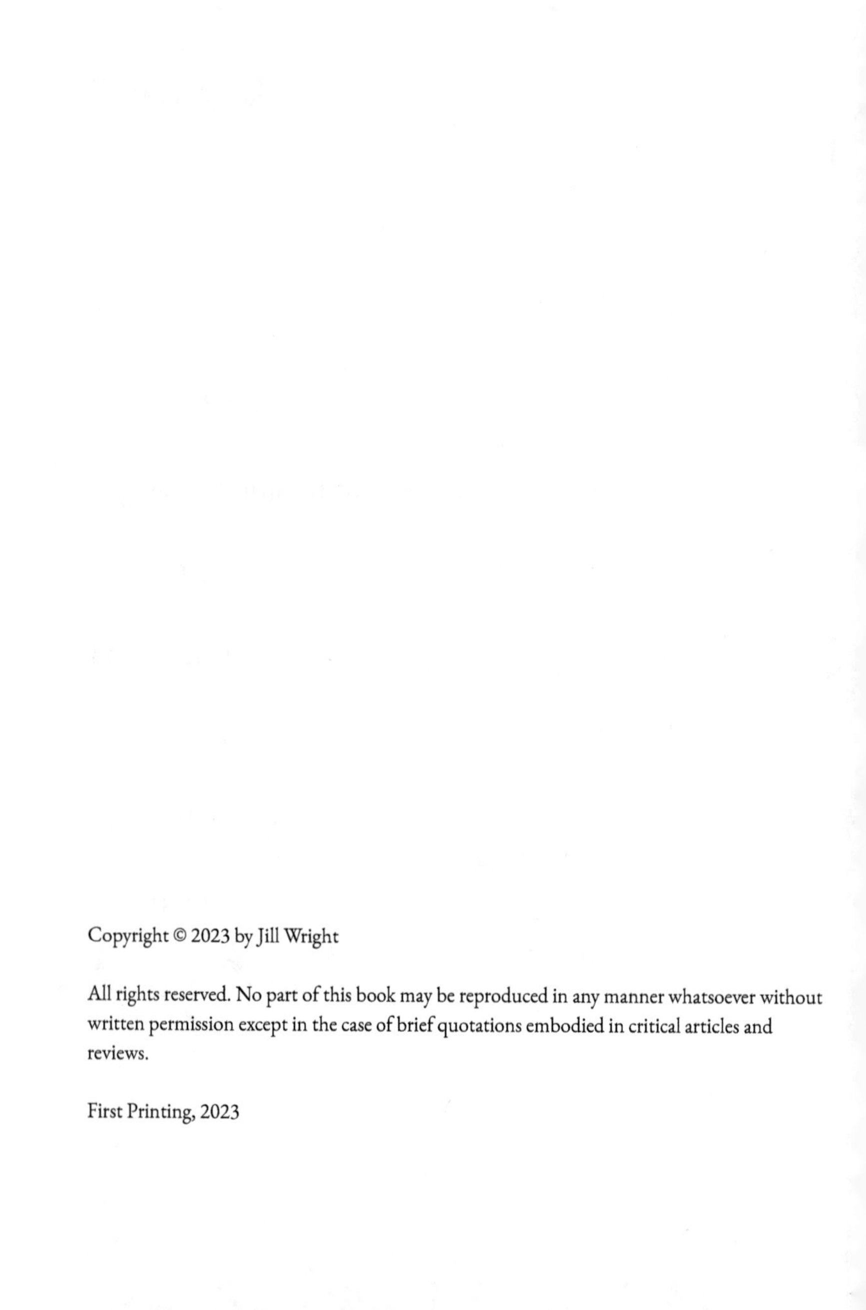



First Printing, 2023

This book is for YOU.

# Author's Note

This book has been a long time in the making. Since I was a young girl, I knew that writing was my calling. I have always felt a sense of wholeness and meaning in helping my community and longed for that to be a driving force in my career. But I did what most of us do and took the road more traveled rather than following my heart. Four years at business school took care of suppressing the creative urge to put pen to paper, and from there I was thrust into the working world where a paycheck was the only thing that mattered. I tried to align my job choices with a component of giving back, but the mounting debt and the stress it was causing always won out.

I found myself in position after position of unsatisfying work that was not utilizing my core strengths and I began to resign myself to life on the hamster wheel. Of hustling to burnout simply to get by. And I was happy enough. That's the insidious problem with following the herd. It's "good enough." It's safe. It's what everyone else is doing. It is what is expected and valued. But it wasn't what my soul truly desired for my time here on Earth. I wasn't fulfilled but I ignored the longing in my heart for many years quite successfully. I built a wonderful life with the man I loved, had a steady career in hospitality, and had a beautiful young family. Like it is for so many of us, on the outside, life was perfect. But the gnawing feeling that I wasn't truly living in alignment never left.

The year 2020 threw me a major curveball and shifted the trajectory of my life completely. Within two years I started a business, navigated the new diagnosis of Autism Spectrum Disorder (ASD) with my eldest child, closed said business (another victim of the pandemic), decided to separate from my husband, sold our family home, started a new job after new job ... all while managing the often-severe symptoms of postpartum depression and anxiety. I pushed myself to complete adrenal burnout. And then I rediscovered personal development. I had always been someone who valued growth and strived to improve. I have very high expectations for myself. In my early twenties, I read Stephen Covey's The 7 Habits of Highly Effective People in my free time and wrote personal mission statements. When the world shut down in March 2020, I reconnected with this practice of curious learning and intentional growth. I started to amass a personal library of self-help books. I found podcasts and thought leaders that inspired me, and I immersed myself in the world of personal growth. I couldn't get enough. I felt like I was finally able to align with my soul again and I knew this was what I had been missing.

In the years since, I have prioritized connecting with myself and worked new habits, routines, and practices into my life that fuel me and make me feel whole. I have found the things that fill my cup so I can pour into others as I so deeply desire to do. As an empath, I had a difficult time protecting my boundaries and would deplete my energy to help and serve others. It's been a long road, but I now have the tools that allow me to be open to connecting and helping others, holding space, and shining light for them without dimming my spirit in the process. I have curated a toolbox of strategies and tactics that serve me daily, that help me to live as the best version of myself so I can live in authenticity and full alignment and show up for others in a way that feeds my soul. I can now meet people where they are and make a difference for them without serving from a place of depletion and emptiness.

The book you are holding is my greatest achievement. It is a collection of the most impactful and life-giving quotes, ideas, practices, habits, tactics, and strategies that I have come across in the past two decades, which I use to create a life that is fully in alignment with my authentic self. In the pages that follow, you will find the tools that have served me in becoming happy, healthy, wealthy, and wise. I am so honoured to share this collection with you and bring this resource into your home. It is my intention for this book to be integrated into your everyday life. For it to live on your bedside table or coffee table and become a go-to tool for you every time you need to reconnect with yourself. I hope you will pick it up when you are feeling a little off, perhaps a little lost, in need of guidance—and also in times when you do feel fully in alignment and are already living in happiness. Let it be a reminder to you, and a valued resource to strengthen and reinforce the connection to your true purpose. This collection of wisdom is intended to support you in leveling up your life in any areas in which you need a bit of a boost. It is my sincere hope and prayer that you find connection and truth within these pages and experience a transformation that exceeds your expectations.

# How to use the Daily Companion Guide

Rather than reading cover to cover, this book is structured as a resource, a companion to your everyday life. You can use it in a variety of ways, whichever feels right for you.

1. Set aside time each morning to read one page. Take five minutes to sit quietly and reflect on the message. Make it your intention to remind yourself of the teaching often throughout the day. Connecting with the feeling and emotion behind the words is the fastest way to create the magic of true transformation.
2. Reach for this book whenever you feel called to do so. Sit with it in your hands and set an intention, aloud or in your mind, to find the message your soul needs to hear. Allow yourself to flip through the pages and land wherever it feels right. Take the wisdom on that page to heart and sit with it for a few minutes, asking yourself how this can serve you where you are in this moment. The process of reflecting on the message and the words is where you will feel your intuition guiding you. Take time to check in with your heart and feel how this lesson can serve you today.
3. Devour it cover to cover! Return to it often to reread or follow one of the rituals above to focus on what your soul most needs to know at any given time.
4. Give a copy of the book to someone you love as a gift. Share this transformative resource with a close friend, a young adult just starting out, a

mother feeling lost in the chaos, or anyone interested in improving their life and finding more happiness, vitality, abundance, and wisdom.

5. Or pick the book up between diaper changes, naps, and laundry. Whatever works for you—this is YOUR experience, after all.

However you choose to use it, I hope this book can truly be a game-changer for you. I can personally attest to the life-changing magic of the tools within, and I am so excited for you to experience the growth and transformation that is possible for you.

*If you are looking for some free resources to get started on your personal growth journey, I invite you to check out* ***jillwright.ca/freebies.***

# Introduction

If you are reading this book, chances are that at some point in your life, you have felt lost, broken, confused, or just plain overwhelmed. Maybe that is how you are feeling right now. Join the club! Welcome. I can guarantee that everyone in your life, and everyone in the world, has been or will be a member of this club at some point in time.

Why? Quite simply: because humans are not perfect. Ever. It is impossible to get through life without having feelings of doubt, insecurity, or just plain madness. But that's okay because we all go through it. Some people are happier, healthier, wealthier, and wiser than the average Jill. That doesn't seem fair, does it? Chances are that you wish you had this kind of magic in your world, the kind that brings happiness and success seemingly without effort.

Well, get ready, my friend, because you are about to learn an empowering fact that will forever change your life: you are in control! YOU can make your life whatever you want it to be! And the best part: it's easy. I'll walk you through it. Don't get me wrong; it's not actually magic, but I have tons of tips and tricks that will help you in achieving everyday happiness.

Before we get started, I'd like to share with you a little about how the idea of this book came to be, and why it's different than other "self-help" books. The main distinction is that this is not actually a self-help book. It's a guide—a collection of tools, tips and tricks, and resources I've learned that have helped me find my personal happiness, and that I hope will inspire you as well. My goal is simply to share my experiences in the hopes that you will take from them what makes sense for you and leave what doesn't. It is not a twelve-step program to becoming a superior human being, or a fool-proof way to find the answers to your most profound questions. It's a road map to navigating the roller coaster of life, as told by someone who has a fair amount of experience in soul-searching.

I am a bona fide inspiration-seeking junkie. And what I have learned through all this self-discovery is that you can drive yourself crazy trying to perfect your "self." A much easier and more rewarding way is to follow your own path! YOU decide what it is that makes you wonderful, what makes you your perfect self. Of course, there are some awesome, life-changing techniques to help, the most powerful of which I will outline in this book, but the real takeaway here is learning how to break free of the "ideal" self and create your own.

My hope is that some of the ideas outlined in the following pages will hit a home run for you, and that after reading it you will feel inspired to make your own happiness and well-being a conscious priority. That you will reflect on and remember the lessons and try to implement them into your life. My suggestion is to choose one idea and start the day with it in mind. Practice your trick throughout the day whenever you think of it, and you will find it becomes a feel-good habit. And when things feel good, we want to do more of it, and it snowballs from there. Trust me, you will slowly become an expert. But I know that as the days go on, and life continues just as it did before you picked up this book, you might slide slowly back into old habits and forget some of what you learned here. That's okay. It happens to me all the time.

Why? We are creatures of habit, and we generally don't make being consciously happy a habit or a priority. We wait for something to happen to us that will make us happy. My point is that only YOU can make you happy, so stop waiting for something or someone else to come along and take the reins. You could be missing out on a whole lot of happy if you keep waiting for it to come to you.

My intention in writing this book is not for you to read it once and have it collect dust on a shelf. This book is intended to be a resource for when you slip and start feeling unhappy, or unfulfilled when you know you need a reminder and a bit of a kick in the pants to get yourself back on track. Or when you have a loved one going through a hard time and the only real help you can offer is some guidance. This guide will be here for you in those inevitable times, and I hope that you underline, highlight, dog-ear, bookmark, or add doodles wherever you find something that hits home for you. Because, trust me, there will be times when you have to grab the dusty book off the shelf and return to it for inspiration and a quick reminder.

The beautiful part about a book like this is that it is universal. Everyone in every place in the world has the power to create their own happiness. It's what connects us as humans but many of us don't realize it. We have the CHOICE to feel happy, sad, or angry. It is something we can control. Not that it's easy; it's not. That's why we aren't already doing it. But the fact that you can learn to control your emotions and, more importantly, your reactions is a beautiful thing. I believe that in general, we all strive for the same things: to be happy, healthy, wealthy, and wise. What will set you apart after reading this book is the knowledge and confidence to take your life back into your own hands and start working towards your goals, whatever the specifics may be. The lessons you will learn are not restricted to a certain gender, a certain age, or a certain nationality or religion. We are all people, and we all want to be happy. And best of all, we can be!

Now, before you ask what authority I have to tell you about being happy, know this: I am not perfect or annoyingly happy, just authentic and genuine. I admit that some days I don't have the energy to try my trusty techniques and I do occasionally succumb to taking a "sick day" to stay in bed in self-pity. But eventually, every time, my head comes out of the fog and these ideas and strategies are always here to help me get quickly back on the track to happiness.

I'm not an expert and I'm not perfect. I've had fleeting moments of success implementing the techniques I am going to show you in this book, and they inspire me. Is it consistent? No. Is it perfect every time? No. But by having the tools and being able to identify where there is room for improvement, I can face each day with the knowledge that I AM in control.

I'm an average person who has put a lot of time and work into finding peace, balance, love, acceptance, and happiness in life. I have sought out, learned, and adapted techniques and tips that have worked for me and compiled them into this book in hopes that it can be a resource for the average person. Whether you are struggling at this moment in time with a tangible challenge, whether you are looking for something more, whether you want to find yourself, or whether you are perfectly content and looking for an inspiring read—or maybe you are looking to educate yourself so you can help someone else find their personal happiness—this book is for YOU.

No one will ever have it all, despite some pretty good attempts to make it appear as if they do (you know the people I'm talking about, and their seemingly perfect lives portrayed through the lens of social media). Making perfection your goal is the surest way to fail in your journey. There is never enough time to accomplish everything you want to do/see/achieve. And isn't that the beauty of life, the sheer brilliance? Because that means you never lose that drive, that ambition, that inspiration to reach for something more. To grow and to develop. Some things will stay on your list forever (for me, that is learning French), and that's okay because in letting some things slide, you have made choices to focus your available time and energy on other important things that can give you the largest return on your investment. And if you find you are stuck in the cycle of spending your time and energy on the "wrong" things and not feeling content, then my hope for you is that this book can guide you to your true path and your true self, and it will become clear for you where your focus should be to start to achieve personal fulfillment in your everyday life, which in turn can lead to a lifetime of happiness.

**Remember, you will always be a work in progress.**

Don't be too hard on yourself. No one is perfect and if you have an off day, then you had an off day. Use it as a reminder to stop, reevaluate if this is really true to your "self," and get back on track! If you decide you've wandered down the wrong footpath, then abandon the day on the side of the road without any hard feelings and try again tomorrow.

# Happy

I consciously started this book with a chapter on happiness because I think it is the fundamental base from which a fulfilled life stems. You can be healthy, wealthy, and wise all you want, but if you are not happy, your life will still feel empty. Happiness is like food for the soul. The more you get, the fuller you become. Too corny? I'll try to tone it down.

I talk a lot about the "self," and you are probably wondering what the heck I mean by that. You may think of yourself in many ways—as a friend, sibling, parent, coworker, or teammate. But none of these titles really and truly gets at the essence of you. That indescribable "-ness" that sums you up entirely. I call it your self, or your soul. A complete picture of everything concrete and intangible about you. Your thoughts, feelings, emotions, faith, intelligence, and beliefs. Your self.

If you pay close attention, your self will always let you know if something is off. It's a tingly feeling that gnaws at you, trying to tell you that something is happening that is blocking your true happiness from being attainable at that time. Listen to this feeling. Learn to recognize it and evaluate what it is that is out of sync with your true self. And make a change because you deserve to always have happiness at the ready!

It's important to know and understand your personal values when you are on a quest to achieve happiness. Values are those intangible things that guide you every day, whether you are aware of them or not. They are ingrained early in your life, and they impact every decision you make, who your friends are, what kind of job you have, and how you spend your time. Each one of us has a unique set of values that we carry with us and use as a reference point. They are the things in life we hold dear, we believe in, that are important to us, and that shape us so significantly. Feeling low? Fake it. Truly.

The physical act of putting a smile on your face can improve your mood. Why? Because the body doesn't know the difference! Smiling sends a signal to your brain that results in the production of dopamine and serotonin, the happy hormones.

The next time you feel a crappy mood coming on, just stop and smile, and see what happens. Make it a habit to smile every time you look in the mirror or make eye contact with someone.

*Start getting happier today! Check out* ***jillwright.ca/freebies*** *for free resources including meditations, EFT tapping sessions, affirmations, workshop replays, book and podcast recommendations and more!*

## *Keep your glass half full*

Positivity is pivotal for happiness.

Positive thinking isn't about ignoring the bad stuff. It's about looking at it through a different lens than you are used to. Instead of hating your body, you can feel grateful that it is still working and functioning after all the crap you've undoubtedly put it through.

Hate your job? Instead of going in every day with a negative attitude, start to focus instead on the outcomes the position is providing you: the income required to sustain your life, the connections you make with colleagues, and the transferrable skills you are acquiring which will help you transition to a role that you can really get excited about.

*Affirmation:*
*I live in a high vibration, and I find it easy to stay there.*

## *What the heck do you WANT?*

Knowing what you want is the very first step to finding happiness. Because how can you find something if you don't know what you are looking for?

Take some time today and sit with yourself quietly. Take a few deep breaths and focus on this question:

**What do I want?**

See what comes up. Your subconscious, your inner knowing, your higher self, your soul—whatever you can relate to in terms of going inward for answers—this place ALWAYS knows.

Your job is to listen.

*Affirmation:*
*I create the life I want to have.*

## *Snap out of it!*

Sometimes, despite our best efforts, we fall back into old habits of negative thinking and actions that make us miserable. That's okay—we're human, after all. The trick is not to get stuck there.

First things first: you need to become aware that you are in that frame of mind. Start acknowledging when you notice yourself slipping into less-than-desirable habits and thought patterns. Then snap out of it! Literally. You can put an elastic band around your wrist and snap yourself as a reminder. The idea isn't to inflict pain, but rather use it as a physical, intentional action that allows a quick break from your current mindset and provides you an opportunity for a reset. The act of snapping the band isn't going to change your mindset for you, though; it's up to you to use the opportunity you've given yourself and make the shift.

Take a few deep breaths. Put a smile on your face. Go for a bathroom break. Get outside for a quick walk. Get some water. Have a snack. It's the action that comes after the snap that's the magic.

> “*Finish each day and be done with it. You have done what you could. Some blunders and absurdities no doubt crept in; forget them as soon as you can. Tomorrow is a new day. You shall begin it serenely and with too high a spirit to be encumbered with your old nonsense.*”
>
> *RALPH WALDO EMERSON*

## *The goal is to feel happy ...*

... so recognize when you are in a negative state and make a conscious effort to change it. YOU are the one with the choice of how you feel, and who wants to feel bad? It's wasted time.

I'm not suggesting that you pretend things are perfect when they aren't, nor am I implying that you can manifest happiness from nowhere. What I want you to realize is that there is always a silver lining, a positive you can focus on. Practice lifting yourself away from the negative and break the habit of getting sucked into it. Practice to find ways that will work for you.

I say work because it IS work! But it's worth it to develop the skills to turn a negative mood, emotion, or situation into a neutral, or a positive. Only you have the power to change your thoughts and emotions, actions, and reactions.

*Affirmation:*
*I will have a good day because it is my choice.*

## *Put a stop to it*

You're walking through your day, minding your own business, and out of nowhere, a barrage of negative thoughts creeps in. Those old familiar thought patterns and stories that your brain is always telling you. "I'm not good enough," "I hate the way I look," "I'm so stupid." Worries creep in without your consent.

Put a stop to it. Imagine a big ol' red stop sign right in front of your face. Close enough that you can't miss it. Picture this stop sign popping into your view every time you get stuck in negative thinking. Let it serve as a jolting reminder that you're going down a rabbit hole and stop yourself before you get consumed. If you can catch yourself before you get buried in the negative thoughts, you stand a chance of switching directions.

This takes practice. Each time you'll catch yourself a bit sooner, and eventually that stop sign is going to pop up all by itself at the onset of a crisis in thinking. Be patient; this tool takes practice and improves with use.

> “*Every master was once a disaster.*”
>
> T. HARV EKER

## Get off autopilot

Doing all the things that require our attention, handling our responsibilities, and, yes, filling any voids with scrolling. It doesn't leave us much time or attention for the things that we like to do. I'm willing to bet that even if I gave you a day off from your life, you wouldn't even know where to start in terms of filling this day with things you enjoy.

Even if it's not realistic to have a day to yourself, it is vital to know what you love doing. To remember what fills your cup and brings you joy. We get so bogged down that we tend to forget the small things we can do to bring a smile to our face.

My challenge to you is to make a love list. Grab a piece of paper and a pen or open that Notes app on your phone and start making a list of all the things you love. Don't limit yourself. Don't question it. Just write it down. Maybe it's a walk in the forest. Maybe it's catching snowflakes with your tongue. Maybe it's cute cat videos. Keep this list handy for a week or so and keep adding to it. Come back to this list every so often to make sure you are incorporating life-giving things into your week.

Maybe you can't visit the zoo, but you can put a picture of a sloth as your computer screen saver. Perhaps fitting a nature walk into your lunch break isn't possible, but what if you switch the location of your Saturday date and go on a hike? Shaping your life around the things that bring you joy is a very effective technique for boosting your happiness. It doesn't need to take more time or energy; it's about being intentional about creating moments of happiness in your every day.

*Affirmation:*
*I create my own path and I walk it with joy.*

*Time isn't something you find.*
*Time is something you make.*

The truth is we have more than enough time. We have the life we have because of how we have decided to spend our time in the past. It's up to us what we spend time on. Yes, you have the constraints of a nine-to-five, and you do need to feed your kids. But—do you need to scroll mindlessly?

Could you instead take that five to ten minutes and call a friend to say hi? Could you listen to your favourite boy band from the '90s on your commute? Can you get someone to watch the kids for an hour so you can get a massage? Is it possible for you to wake up 15 minutes earlier and read that book that's been on your nightstand for a year now?

*Affirmation:*
*I have more than enough time to do everything I want to do.*

## *Make time for what you love to do*

Weekly planning isn't usually the first thing that comes to mind when you are talking about happiness but hear me out. If you look at your upcoming week and you don't see something that is FUN, you're doing it wrong. And hey, no blame or shame or shade, or whatever the kids are saying these days. It happens to all of us grown-ups. We forget the fun! Because let's be honest—life fills with obligations like work and parenting, and then we are too exhausted to do anything but binge on the couch.

What if you intentionally built fun into your weekly schedule and treated it like an obligation? What if it was a nonnegotiable like going to work? You might still find yourself tapped out at the end of the day with a glass of wine and a bag of chips in bed, but you just might find that you have a little extra pep in your step because you prioritized fun. But wait, where exactly are you supposed to fit this fun into your already jam-packed calendar? Good question. The answer: anywhere you freaking want.

If you need to, schedule it in your calendar. Whether it's a cousins' movie night, a wine-and-cheese party, or a walk in the woods, be sure to make the time to do the things that bring you joy, because life can get so busy, and the days fill up fast. If we aren't intentional about how we fill our time, it slips away from us. So go ahead and grab your calendar and schedule your favourite activities for the next month.

If you can book one activity a week that brings you joy, from a massage to an hour alone to read, you're winning. Just be sure to treat it like you would any other commitment on your calendar and SHOW UP when you said you would. It's easy to bail on ourselves—don't be that person.

As the years go on and the responsibilities pile up, fun seems to always take a back seat. Whether that's intentional or not, it happens to the best of us.

I think it's time we pulled our old friend fun out from the back of the closet, dusted her off, and took her out for a date. Adding fun back into your week is a surefire way to increase your happiness.

Since fun is always better with friends, grab a gal pal and catch the latest chick flick together on a school night. Or bring your bestie with you to the mall when it's time to update your wardrobe. Having the spirit of fun and someone to share it with is all you need—the activity doesn't even matter that much if the intention is there.

All I'm saying is that if you put it in your planner and treat fun as an obligation, you're more likely to find creative ways of fitting it in. And who doesn't want more fun in their life?

*Affirmation:*
*I choose where to spend my energy.*

## *There is nothing like a good belly laugh*

The kind that you need to catch your breath from. That makes tears roll down your cheeks. Laughter is so healing for us because it increases our intake of oxygen, stimulating endorphins in our brain. Laughter reduces our stress response and calms our nervous system. Our heart rate and blood pressure decrease when we laugh. Our circulation gets better, and our muscles relax. According to the Mayo Clinic, this is real physical stuff that happens to our bodies when we partake in a good giggle.

The cumulative effect is even more powerful. Long-term benefits of laughing include an improved immune system, pain relief, and improvements in your mood. So go ahead and schedule a date with that friend who always cracks you up. Pop on your favourite funny movie or go to a comedy club. Even looking at comics or memes that make you chuckle will reap benefits.

They say laughter is the best medicine. And we brush it off because we tend to think of medicine as pills and prescriptions, something that comes from outside ourselves. But what if we had the power to heal ourselves from within by doing something that feels amazing?

*When you control your mindset, you can choose how you approach every single situation you come across*

Traffic doesn't have to be rage-inducing if you approach it from the perspective that it allows a bit more time in your day to listen to that podcast. A rude comment doesn't have to rattle you when you look at it through the lens of knowing it's not actually about you, but truly a projection from the person who said it. When you consciously control your mindset and perspective, you can go through life making the best decisions possible. When you're confident that you are making the right choices and are in control of your mindset, guilt has no power.

Maybe this sounds too good to be true. Maybe you've tried hippie-dippy positive self-talk or affirmations before, but it just didn't work, or you didn't stick with it. I know it's hard. It takes practice but the end results are so worth it.

*Take a minute and be honest. What mindset are you currently in? Do you feel like things are out of your control and nothing can be changed? Or do you have dreams and goals for yourself that would require some effort, but you believe are in your reach?*

## *An attitude of gratitude*

It's actually not woo-woo, and it's harder than you think. Gratitude takes practice, and you can strengthen your gratitude muscles with a bit of effort. The trick with this one is challenging yourself to feel gratitude for the small things. It's not about pretending things are all roses when they are actually garbage. Rather, it's consciously looking for the things you can appreciate and be grateful for, even in (and especially in) the hard times and less-than-perfect scenarios.

Besides actively looking for and appreciating things in real time, another way to practice gratitude is to develop a nightly practice. As you crawl into bed each night, try to recall three things that happened that day, between getting out of bed and getting back in, that you can be grateful for, even if you didn't feel it in the moment. The hot cup of coffee. The text from a friend that made you smile. They don't have to be big things, and in fact, it's better if they aren't because that means you are digging deeper than being grateful for the obvious: your house and your family, and your job. The point is to look for the little things to be grateful for. The most important part of this practice is to smile and replay the feeling in your mind as you are identifying it.

When you start looking for things to be grateful for, you start to be able to feel and appreciate the small things as you experience them. And as you practice this, the universe/God/source/whatever you believe in will send you more things to be grateful for. Like attracts like, after all.

"*Trade your expectations for appreciation and your whole world changes in an instant.*"

*TONY ROBBINS*

## *Keep happiness close at hand*

Literally. I want you to start a collection of things that make you smile (cute animal videos, pics of family and friends, good songs, etc.). This can be a file on your computer, or a shoebox in your closet with photographs and mix tapes. The point is to have a collection of things that either make you happy or represent a time when you experienced joy.

Put in the tickets from that baseball game when you caught a fly ball or save an image of the team. Having a place to go to when you need a happiness boost is not only convenient but a surefire way to improve your mood when you're feeling down and out.

*Don't wait! Go dig out a shoe box and create a happiness shrine.*

## *Give yourself a compliment every day*

It's okay to admit that your hair looks phenomenal or that you make a mean beef stew. Because let's be honest; compliments from others are few and far between. They shouldn't be so hard to come by, but honestly, who needs external validation? Be your own cheerleader.

Recognizing and acknowledging things that you rock at and reminding yourself of them often is an awesome way to boost your confidence and your spirits.

The stories we tell ourselves become our reality, and because the sub-conscious mind can't tell the difference between what's real and happening in front of us, and what we think and imagine, you can even sneak in a few compliments that aren't 100% true, YET.

*Affirmation:*
*"I am amazing at__________ (fill in the blank)."*

## *Have a daily mantra*

A short phrase that you can say to yourself or think on repeat. Can you guess what mine is? Look no further than the title of this book: I am happy, healthy, wealthy, and wise. I expanded on the well-known quote from Benjamin Franklin "Early to bed and early to rise makes a man healthy, wealthy, and wise" because I thought happiness was a worthy objective and really shouldn't be overlooked!

Repeat your mantra to yourself throughout the day when you want to help focus your mind and body on the moment. Say your mantra to yourself when you look in a mirror. When you are walking the dog or doing the dishes. Speak it out loud after your nightly gratitude practice. Let your mantra become ingrained in your day because the more you repeat it, the stronger it becomes.

*Mantras to try:*
*I am happy. I am healthy. I am wealthy. I am wise.*
*Everything is always working out for me.*
*My life is unfolding in divine order.*
*The universe has my back.*

## *Enjoy the small things*

This feels like a cliché but there's a reason that clichés exist—because they're true! If you can turn your attention to the smaller details, the things you might normally overlook, you can start to find enjoyment everywhere.

Go ahead and smell those daisies. Take a few extra minutes to enjoy the smell of your favourite soap as you wash your hands. And most definitely gaze upon the splendor that is a magnificent sunset. Noticing and appreciating the small delights in life costs nothing and adds tremendous happiness opportunities throughout the day.

*Affirmation:*
*I take a deep breath and center myself in the present moment.*

## *Just as important as what to do is what NOT to do*

Try not to allow negative things or people to take up your thoughts, time, energy, or emotion. If something isn't for you, or upsets you, or creates feelings of anxiety, stress, or sadness, simply acknowledge that you don't want those feelings in your life and move on.

The biggest mistake you can make is to get bogged down in the negative things because it is like quicksand and is such a hard mind frame to break out of. Protect your high vibes with all your might!

*Affirmation:*
*I choose happiness right here, right now.*

## *Find what makes you happy*

My friends call me Grandma because I love history. When I went to Scotland, I spent my time in castles and museums, and I enjoy spending time researching my ancestors. I go to bed early and enjoy talking with older people. I love their experience and wisdom. I love the bygone eras, the culture, and the traditions.

I don't get offended that people think my habits and interests are kooky; they are just more things that make me unique and make me happy. So why would I stop simply because other people in my life have different interests?

Follow your unique passions. The beauty of the world is that we are each unique, and if we lose touch with what makes us unique, we lose touch with ourselves and our mission, our purpose, and our path/journey. Don't be embarrassed by your interests; the world needs diversity and there is sure to be a group of people interested in the same things you are.

*Don't worry about being someone others want to be around. Be someone YOU want to be around.*

## *Purge your friend list (on social media, or in real life)*

Don't waste time on people or things that bring you down, or that don't add value and joy to your life. How you spend your time and whom you spend it with shapes your life dramatically. Many personal development experts say that you become a combination of the five people you spend the most time with. You take on the traits, mindset, and attitudes of those close to you. So be careful who you allow into your inner circle!

Do those close to you light you up, fill your cup, and make you laugh? Or do you feel heavy, anxious, or even depleted after an interaction? Paying attention to how we feel during and after an interaction, even an online one, can tell us a lot about which relationships are serving us, and which ones it's time to put on the back burner (or unfollow).

*Affirmation:*
*I surround myself with fun people and things that light me up and give my soul energy. And if my table is empty, I enjoy my own company, because I am awesome.*

## *Whenever somebody pops into your head, send them a quick note to let them know you're thinking about them*

It's usually not a coincidence, especially if you think of them several times over a short period of time.

It doesn't have to be a long phone call or email, just a quick text or voice note to let them know you're thinking about them goes a long way in fostering your important relationships. Research shows that relationships are one of the key contributing factors to a happy life, so you definitely don't want to skip this one.

*Affirmation:*
*I create happy, sustainable relationships with people who make my heart smile.*

## *Kick guilt to the curb*

Start by being honest with yourself about why something is making you feel guilty. Guilt is usually based on what you believe others will think of your decision and or actions.

I'm here to tell you: what others think of you is none of your business.

You do you! And own it. Fully accept that the choices you make are for your highest good and stick with them.

> "*Don't mask yourself as a horse when you know you are a unicorn.*"
>
> LISA NICHOLS

## *Nothing is fixed*

People with a growth mindset believe they can change and improve. They don't fear failure because they know they can learn, and through hard work and training become better. They don't fear the struggle of trying something new because they know they can grow. The struggle is seen as part of the process.

On the other hand, those with a fixed mindset are stuck where they are. They don't see opportunities and feel like life is never going to change.

Here's a secret, though: YOU are the one deciding which mindset you have.

Yes, you read that right: **you get to decide.**

So which mindset are you currently in? Which do you want to be in? Staying in a growth mindset takes practice if you have been stuck in a fixed mindset for some time. But it's worth the work to shift it. Imagine all the ways your life could change for the better if you simply acknowledged it was possible.

When we open our minds to possibilities that we believe can exist for us, we start to see those opportunities all around us. If you take small action steps towards these new opportunities, you will soon find your life IS changing for the better. Then you will have proof ... and the growth mindset will firmly take hold.

> “ *The only way you fail is if you give up.* ”
>
> *UNKNOWN*

## *Happiness comes when aligned action is taken toward your dreams*

All that's standing between your current situation and your ideal future, where you'd go for it and kill your goal, is the belief that you can do it, and the conviction to keep putting in the work, day after day, until you get there.

You're already ahead of the game if you know what you want from life, so GO GET IT.

*Affirmation:*
*Watch me as I make amazing things happen, even more amazing than the things that have already happened.*

## *Ask for what you want and need*

We often assume others intuitively know what we want and need from them. But let's be honest: there are no mind readers here. Putting that kind of pressure on someone else to instinctively know what you need is not fair to them, and not fair to you because you're unlikely to get the results you want.

It doesn't have to be impolite or bossy to ask for what you want. Start small, with someone you love and trust. Needing some comfort? Ask for a hug. When the inevitable "What should we do for dinner?" comes up at 4 p.m. and you just need the other person to make the decision today, tell them.

Soon you'll build up the confidence to start expressing your needs and wants to your friends, your coworkers, and your kids. If you can master the art of politely and firmly expressing what you want, you are going to start getting it. And imagine how your life will look then!

*Affirmation:*
*I am conquering my fears and becoming stronger each day.*

## *Compare each decision against your values and priorities*

Is it aligned? Does it feel right? Knowing that will make it easy for the answer to be a HECK YES or a HECK NO.

Whenever you are presented with an offer, an opportunity, or a request, simply ask yourself if you want to do the thing.

If the answer isn't a resounding heck yes, then it must be a no. It's that simple. If you aren't jumping up and down at the thought of being a bridesmaid or baking cookies for the bake sale, say no.

Be ruthless and understand the opportunity cost of saying yes to something that isn't aligned, or will take your precious time, energy, or money away from something you truly care about.

Look at every aspect of your day and week. Look at your relationships and commitments. Categorize everything into a heck yes or a heck no. Craft your life around the things and people that are a heck yes for you. Do not waste any more time, energy, or money on a heck no.

> “ *To be unclear is to be unkind.* ”
>
> BRENÉ BROWN

## *Saying no doesn't have to be painful*

I know you probably already feel anxious just thinking about that two-letter word. I was the same. I wanted to puke when I imagined the scenario of saying no to someone for the first time. When I actually did say it, my heart was pounding out of my chest! But guess what? The world didn't fall apart, and no one yelled at me.

If you can say no firmly and politely, with respect and confidence, then most reasonable people won't even bat an eyelash.

> "*Everything will be okay in the end. If it is not okay, then it is not yet the end.*"
>
> THE BEST EXOTIC MARIGOLD HOTEL MOVIE

*A super quick way to reframe your mindset, and therefore your outcome, is to add the word "yet"*

"I haven't reached the level of income I want. Yet."
"I haven't found the love of my life. Yet."
"I haven't hit XYZ goal. Yet."

See how that one little word completely changes EVERYTHING?

*Affirmation:*
*My best days are ahead of me.*

## *Have your indulgences without guilt*

The entire point of an indulgence is to feel good, right? So, it stands to reason that it will completely defeat the purpose of indulging yourself if you immediately feel guilty about it afterward.

Try something different. Next time you treat yourself to dessert at a restaurant, stay up a bit too late watching a show you adore, or lose track of time scrolling a gorgeous Pinterest account, instead of chastising yourself for a "bad" decision, try accepting that no one is perfect, and we all deserve an indulgence now and again.

> "*Everything in moderation, including moderation.*"
>
> *OSCAR WILDE*

## *Do you have a Thrive List?*

A Thrive List is a resource you can utilize in those moments when you feel low, blah, or bored.

It's super easy and fun to create. Carve out ten minutes and grab a piece of paper and a pen. Put on your favourite song in the background and brain dump onto the paper everything you can think of that makes you feel amazing. This could be a bubble bath or a spontaneous weekend getaway. It could be a phone call with a loved one or a night out dancing. The goal here is to come up with as many things as you can that light you up and make you feel alive.

Not feeling inspired? Ask your family and friends what they would put on your Thrive List. Or take a week and commit to noticing the moments when you feel amazing. Add them to the list! Once you have it, take a picture of the Thrive List and keep it saved on your phone. Put the actual written list somewhere you can see it often: your bedside table or in the bathroom, or kitchen. Tuck it inside your agenda; whatever works for you.

When you are feeling off or you're having a pity party or you're just plain sad, you can revisit this list and choose something to get excited about. Use it like a menu and take action towards something that will get you excited, and then watch your mood transform!

# *Keep moving forward*

Your personal "why" is a deep motivation that fuels everything you do. It's what keeps you moving forward in life. Often, when we feel overwhelmed, anxious, or depressed, it's because our current situation doesn't align with our why – the reason we want what we want.

To be truly happy, it is of utmost importance that you dig deep to find your why and use it as a lighthouse to keep you on course with what is important to you in your life.

Everything you desire is within your reach. Is it going to be easy to get it? No. Anything worth having takes hard work and patience to achieve. But knowing you can have whatever your heart desires is pretty darn good motivation for putting one foot in front of the other every day and showing up as your best self.

If you feel like you don't have time, in fact what you don't have is clarity. Focus on WHERE you want to go, and WHY. Having a compelling future in mind can make all the difference when you feel like you don't have time to take on something new, work towards a goal, etc.

*Affirmation:*
*Micro wins build momentum. Momentum is the key to success.*

## *It's true when they say you get what you give*

If you're feeling like you could use a boost, a helping hand, or even just some community, why not try turning the tables?

Offer a smile to a stranger, donate some groceries to your local food bank, or even just get online and share a friend's business with your personal network.

Doing something nice for someone else not only brings you a sense of joy and fulfillment, but others notice—and they start to do nice things for you. This, my friends, is the circle of life.

*Who can you surprise and inspire today?*

## *Do more of what you love*

We have all heard the phrase, "If you love what you do, you'll never work a day in your life." While this may be true, not all passions pay the bills. And sometimes we aren't particularly talented at the things we love to do.

Instead, decide if you want your passion, that thing you love to do, to be your career, OR a primary focus in your personal life. Is it a job or a hobby? If you can earn a living from it, FANTASTIC. Go do that. But even if the opportunity to support yourself financially by doing something you love doesn't exist, you can still prioritize that passion in other ways and other areas of your life.

The point here is to do more of what you love to do. Period.

*Work harder on yourself than you do at your job.*

## *What are some words that make you happy?*

Words that inspire you or stir something up in your soul? Write them down and put them somewhere that's visible throughout the day.

Whether it's a sticky note that you put on the fridge, a notecard with beautiful writing attached to your bathroom mirror, or even a collage of cut-out magazine letters pieced together that you tape to the front of your notebook like in middle school. Having these powerful words visible throughout the day means you will consciously or unconsciously pay attention to them. And filling your brain with words that inspire you and create joy is a surefire way to boost your happiness on the daily.

*Affirmation:*
*I am worthy of an exceptional life.*

## *Visualize your compelling future!*

Take five minutes, get quiet, and daydream. Imagine in vivid detail what you want out of life in general, or in a particular situation. Get super specific and really feel the emotions behind what you are imagining. Whenever you find yourself feeling a dip in positivity or needing a boost, come back to this place and this feeling.

Or maybe you would prefer to grab a few friends and spend an afternoon making vision boards.

This takes a bit of prep work (making a life list, finding words and images that support that vision) but if you come prepared, it's a breeze. Do it old school with magazine cut-outs, digitally using a Pinterest board, or create it in Canva.

Choose a vision that's three months, one year, or even five years down the road. The goal is to have fun, get creative, and let your imagination run wild.

Create a vision board that represents your dream life and keep it somewhere you can see it every day. Take a few minutes to really look at it, feel the emotions behind your dreams, and commit to taking one action step every day to get yourself closer to this reality.

Bonus points if you get together with the same friends after the three months, one year, five years, and reflect on the vision boards to see what came to fruition!

## *Start your day as a champion rather than on defense*

Let's face it; mornings are hard, and they set the tone for your day. We often wake up unrested and usually to an alarm or to a screaming kid. Not exactly a peaceful way to start your day. But what if you could set yourself up so mornings were restorative? What if you could start your day feeling motivated, ready, and excited?

You can. You just need to change the way you think about it! The first thing is to create a morning routine (or a night routine, if you have kids that wake up with the birds like mine do). Create the habit of doing a few things every night before bed (or first thing in the morning if you have some alone time) that will set you up for a less stressful morning. Run the dishwasher, practice gratitude, or do some yoga. Write in your journal, get the lunches ready, or meditate. Whatever it is that helps you feel prepared and ready to take on the day.

*Before you get out of bed, ask yourself 3 questions:*

*What can I get excited about today?*
*How will I handle it if (when) things go sideways?*
*Who can I help/inspire today?*

# *Create a Results List*

This is NOT a to-do list.

This is a list of one to three things that you can commit to achieving today.

What are the results you want?

*Affirmation:*
*I am achieving my dreams every day.*

## *Train yourself to focus on the positive*

This is something that does take practice so don't be too hard on yourself if it takes some time to get there. Go day by day.

When you catch yourself spiraling into negative thinking, try to flip the script:

- What is there to gain?
- What went right?
- How can this be happening FOR me?
- Is there a silver lining?
- What is this trigger trying to teach me?

If you look hard enough there is always a positive—even if it's simply a hard lesson that you needed to learn.

*Affirmation:*
*My failures don't disqualify me from moving forward with positive momentum.*

## *Keeping a good balance is key*

Find a balance between focusing on yourself (introverts are best at this because they are fueled by internal energy) and focusing on the outside world (extroverts naturally gain their energy from outside sources so this comes more easily for them).

It's the yin and the yang.

Each of us has a natural preference for social events or solitude, but what if you tried to go outside your comfort zone now and again? You might just find that happiness comes from unexpected places.

" *Balance is a verb.* "

*JAMIE GLOWACKI*

## *Emotions are contagious*

Have you ever noticed how if you spend time around someone who is positive, energetic, and upbeat, you start to feel better? And likewise; how the life gets sucked out of you when you are around someone who is in a bad mood, or a person who is negative, judgmental, or mean?

As humans, we pick up on the energetic signals of emotions in others, so be careful of whom you spend your time with. Take note after an interaction whether you feel uplifted or drained. Choose to spend your time with the people who lift you up.

We all have those coworkers whose negative attitude brings the whole office down, so if you simply can't escape the bad attitude, build yourself a metaphoric bubble. Picture a glass dome around you, or a big bubble surrounding your entire body. Other people's emotions can't get through this bubble and impact you. This is a super (if a bit woo-woo) way to protect your energy and emotions in situations like family gatherings you must attend, and may even want to attend, but you don't love how you feel during or after the event. Protect yourself!

*Have a walk, have a cry, have a sleep. Not necessarily in that order.*

## *If you have this book in your hands, you are in the upper echelon of society*

You have someone who loves you who bought you this book. Or you had the means to purchase it. Or you live in a place where there is a library, and you have access to transportation to get there. You have friends from whom you heard about the book, or you have access to the internet and learned about it online. Upper echelon.

We can sometimes lose sight of the fact of just how privileged we really are. This is not a PSA to "save the starving children in Africa," but it is a reminder to appreciate what you have, rather than focusing on what you don't.

It's a simple concept that should come as no surprise; we have all heard it before. But have you ever really practiced it? Taken it into account consciously? Appreciating the things and opportunities that you have, big and small, is a way to bring gratitude into your heart, and when you live in a place of gratitude, happiness naturally follows.

*Will the version of you 10 years from now be proud of what you're doing?*

## *Borrow their joy instead of letting it dim your light*

Sometimes jealousy and envy sneak in. I get it. It's totally normal - they are legitimate emotions. Don't try to squash them, but instead notice when you feel them pop up and try to flip the switch on them.

A good example I can share from my own life is when I was experiencing fertility issues when trying to start my family. Every time I saw a pregnant person, I would feel worse about my struggle. When I saw mamas playing with their babies, I felt jealous. As my friends were all getting pregnant, it took everything I had not to cry tears of sadness for myself instead of celebrating their joy. I got swallowed up in it.

Until one day, when I decided to try being happy for them. Celebrate wholeheartedly with them. Acknowledge the emotions their situation was bringing up for me, but also remind myself that their situation didn't impact or change mine at all. It took practice, but as I was able to genuinely work toward feeling joy and happiness for these women, I was able to release a bit of angst, anger, and shame.

That's where the magic is—being able to feel happiness for other people's experiences.

*Every sixty seconds you spend upset is one minute of happiness you'll never get back.*

## You are who you are

Too often we say: "I'll be happy when __________." Fill in the blank. When I have that job, when I earn that income, when this challenge is over, etc.

Simply getting to the next step isn't going to magically bring you happiness. The key is to accept and appreciate where you are right now. Because all you have is right now.

Let's be honest; if you aren't fulfilled with yourself and your life at this stage, it's not the money, the job, the family, or the accolades that are going to bring you the happiness you are after. It's not a given that what you think you want will bring you the joy you are looking for. Stop seeking it externally and start looking inward.

Making peace with who you are and where you are, and really getting comfortable in your own skin is the answer. If you can be happy with where you are and what you have now, at this moment, you've won. You're ahead of the game. And honestly, you will start to see your goals and dreams materialize a lot faster because you are working toward them from a place of joy and fulfillment, not scarcity and lack.

*Affirmation:*
*This, or something better.*

# Healthy

What does health mean to you? For me, when I refer to health, I'm referring to the things that can rejuvenate the body and mind. Not just physical health in the form of lack of pain and dis-ease, but proactive health inside and out. Health isn't so much about what you look like on the outside but more about how you feel on the inside. It's energetics.

Energetics doesn't have to be all about high vibes, although that certainly is a nice side effect of feeling healthy and strong in your body and mind. Energetics is also about calm, and stillness. It's the anxiety (or lack thereof), the determination of spirit, the lightheartedness. It's about how you FEEL. If we are intentional about feeling good in our bodies and minds, we can create a life that is beyond our wildest imagination.

We've all heard the advice: don't sweat the small stuff and probably read the book by Richard Carlson. When you break it down, here is what this really means:

The "sweat" piece is referring to your body's stress response. When we feel stressed and our nervous system gets in fight-or-flight mode we experience many physical changes, which include increased perspiration. The body is getting ready to run from a metaphorical saber-toothed tiger, even if the stressor is simply a traffic jam. The body doesn't know the difference; it just feels the stress, and we respond as we were evolutionarily designed to: fight or flight. This is a response that served humans well in the past. Either you got away, or you got eaten. Either way, the increased heart rate, anxiety, and perspiration was short-lived.

In today's world, we still have that same innate response, but we have so many more stressors than our prehistoric ancestors. Our bodies are constantly in fight-or-flight mode, which is causing havoc for our health. The list of physical and mental problems that are caused by prolonged stress is endless. One way to combat this is to literally not sweat the small stuff.

Instead of having a stress response to every hiccup in your day, try a different strategy, such as taking some deep belly breaths, turning on your favourite song and singing as loud as you can, or shifting your focus to three things you are grateful for. These strategies are quick and free, and with practice can totally transform your habitual reaction to small stressors and tremendously improve your health and wellness.

*Learn more about energetics by checking out* ***jillwright.ca/freebies*** *for free resources including meditations, EFT tapping sessions, affirmations, workshop replays, book and podcast recommendations and more!*

## *Try yoga*

It's the 21st century—if you haven't ever done yoga, what are you waiting for?

There have been so many nights when yoga breathwork and poses have saved me from anxiety and insomnia. If you practice yoga during the day, you get the instant benefits of relaxation, clarity of thought, and mindfulness.

Grab a friend and get to a class. Or turn on your phone and follow along with a free class online. You don't even need a mat. Just start and feel the stress melt away.

*Repeat after me: Ommmmm.*

## *Make sleep your secret weapon*

Having enough sleep can set you up for success in all the roles you play, allow you to better control your mindset, stay calm and energized, and deal with all the crap that gets thrown at you on the daily. Taking the time to ensure you're rested means that you can be focused, intentional, and energetic with the time you are awake. You can get more done in less time when you are well-rested. It's the antidote to burnout.

There is some controversy about the benefits of naps and how they can impact night sleep, but for me (and I would argue for all parents of kids under five), naps are a must. They must be prioritized and treated with reverence. Try taking a forty-five-minute nap (no longer) when you need a refresh. Be sure to wake up at least seven hours before you intend to fall asleep for the night and you will get all the benefits of a nap (increased focus and alertness, improved mood, quicker reaction time, better memory, etc.) without sacrificing quality of overnight sleep. Win-win.

Making sure you have enough sleep is going to ensure your body and brain are fully revved up and capable of making smart decisions. It gives you the patience to interact with your family, coworkers, and other humans, and it is the absolute best form of self-care that exists. Think about it: it's free, you don't need any equipment to do it, and there's no training involved. How are more people not doing this?

> “*Sleep is an actual nutrient.*”
>
> *JAMIE GLOWACKI*

## *You need an Attitude Adjustment (Playlist)*

It's exactly like it sounds. Create a playlist on Spotify (or even a good-ole mixtape) with your favourite tunes and pop it on shuffle whenever you are feeling stressed or notice yourself unraveling.

It's especially useful on those days when you wake up on the wrong side of the bed and nothing is right, no one is right, and you're crabby no matter what. You know the mood—we've all been there. The best part of this quick tool is that within minutes, you'll be singing or dancing along and that is the magic. Vocal expression—yelling or singing—and movement like jumping or dancing physically shifts you out of your current rotten mood and into a more positive and energetic state.

Seriously. I hereby challenge you to make your own Attitude Adjustment Playlist. Make sure you add songs that pump you up, touch your soul, and make you sing out loud. Put on as many songs as you want, but I'm willing to bet that you'll only need two or three to get back to being your best self.

*Affirmation:*
*My vibration is high. I attract good energy.*

## *Don't depend on willpower alone*

An action becomes a habit once it is in the domain of your subconscious mind. This means you don't need to think about it, you just do it. We can use this to our advantage with habit formation.

Have you ever arrived home without really paying attention to the drive? You got there on autopilot. That's because you had done the same drive so many times before that your conscious mind didn't need to think about it. Your subconscious mind took over and you just did it.

Trying to add a new habit to your life through willpower alone can be difficult and time-consuming. You need to rely on internal motivation, which you don't always have at the ready. Make it easier on yourself and get the action on autopilot.

Try a method called habit stacking. Simply add a new habit to one you already do. By stacking a new habit on top of an existing habit you take advantage of a built-in cue, or trigger, to perform the new habit. And because the existing habit is done daily, you ensure yourself repetition and consistency which accelerate the process of moving your new action from the conscious mind to the subconscious mind.

Practice gratitude while you brush your teeth. Have a glass of water as your coffee is brewing.

*Consistency builds confidence and gets results.*

## *Identify things that you can decide on ONCE and never have to think about it again*

This can be something like making Friday night "pizza night", doing your groceries on Monday afternoons, or always wearing a dress on Wednesdays. You get the idea.

Your ability to make good decisions deteriorates with the number of decisions you make. On average, adults make 35,000 decisions PER DAY. That is outrageous. We are not even conscious of many of these decisions. It stands to reason that with this many choices each day, your ability to handle decisions is impeded.

Decision fatigue is a real problem in our modern world. Even the seemingly insignificant decisions we make daily add up and can zap our precious energy and brain power. Do yourself a solid and set some standards for yourself so you can free up that beautiful brain to focus on more important things than what's for dinner.

*Affirmation:*
*Decisions come easily to me.*

## *Get in flow*

The popular meditation app Headspace defines flow state as "that sense of fluidity between your body and mind, where you are totally absorbed by and deeply focused on something, beyond the point of distraction. Time feels like it has slowed down. Your senses are heightened. You are at one with the task at hand, as action and awareness sync to create an effortless momentum." You'll often hear athletes talking about flow state when they say they're "in the zone."

We can all achieve this if we pay attention to how we feel when we perform certain tasks and honour that. Maybe it makes sense for you to work out in the morning when you have tons of energy and save your evenings for writing because that's when you feel most creative. It's a total game changer when you can leverage the time of day you feel most productive and focused to work on your important tasks.

Super important, though: if you aren't feeling it, just stop. There's no point in forcing the work if your head and heart aren't in it. Come back to the task another time and instead use your less focused moments for less important chores.

*Affirmation:*
*Energy flows through me.*

## Meditate

Meditation is the fastest, cheapest, and most accessible way to deal with anxiety that I know of.

Don't worry; we all suck when we first start. It takes some practice. But if you keep at it, you get better and you can quickly slip into a relaxed and calm state.

Try sitting or lying down with your eyes closed. Take three deep breaths in through your nose and out through your mouth. Sit for a minute and just focus on your breathing. What the breath feels like coming in and going out. You're gonna have thoughts—let them be. Come back to focusing on your breathing. That's it.

I highly recommend listening to a guided meditation. Personally, this is something I have worked into my nighttime routine. There are some great apps and podcasts available, so try a few out and see what you like best. Some days it centers me, and some days I fidget and let my mind run free instead of focusing on the meditation at hand. But I am always grateful I took the time to do it. Being mindful is a sneaky skill that builds up and strengthens you without you even realizing it.

*Try it for one minute a day. Then two minutes. Work your way up to ten minutes a day.*

## You have to put the work in

Hard work is the price of admission for a memorable life.

Do the work, eat the greens, and move your body. Doing the hard things now will ensure that you have an easier life later.

Doing the easy things now (sitting on the couch, eating out, binge-watching Netflix) will set you up for a harder life later.

*Affirmation:*
*I am strong and capable of great things.*

## *Create some energy!*

Energy isn't something that just comes to you—you make it. Go ahead and dance, sing, jump, work out, stretch—whatever makes you come alive. Move your body for a few minutes to get that energy flowing.

Energy is the most important ingredient for life and success.

> “ *The power plant does not have energy, it generates it.* ”
>
> BRENDON BURCHARD

## *Be kind*

Dr. David R. Hamilton teaches us that "kindness practices can improve our mental health by boosting happiness, creating resilience to stress, and protecting against depression."

It stands to reason that being kind is important for your health.

Being kind to YOURSELF gives you the extra benefits of being the giver and the receiver of kindness.

*The golden rule: Do unto others as you would have them do unto you.*

# *The way you talk to yourself matters*

Pay attention to the words in your head when you get dressed, when you look in the mirror, when you mess something up, and when you do something right.

Are you your own worst critic? Do you tell yourself stories about why you aren't good enough? Do you give yourself the credit you deserve?

The words and thoughts we have around our self-image matter more than you might think. They make up the narrative we believe and therefore that our subconscious mind tries to make a reality for us.

Don't have the life you want yet? Try changing the way you speak to yourself and watch what happens.

*It isn't always enough to be forgiven by others. Sometimes, you must learn to forgive yourself.*

## *Know your limits and when to ask for help*

None of us can do it all. We aren't meant to.

As humans, we live in a society in which we rely on each other to fulfill various roles to keep our world functioning smoothly.

So why would you think you need to do it all yourself and, on top of that, do it perfectly? No one is expecting that of you.

Become aware of your upper limits. Know when you are taking on too much or coming close to burnout, and tag someone else in to help carry the load.

> “*It takes a village to raise a child.*”
>
> UNKNOWN

## *Move your body*

Physical movement is not only good for your body but great for your mind and soul. When you exercise you are getting the blood pumping, oxygen flowing, and muscles active. We know that. But did you also know you are moving energy around your body? Allowing blocked negative energy and emotions to move out?

Dance your heart out, take a walk on your lunch break, or climb with your kids at the playground. Take up a team sport or even just stretch in your living room.

Harvard research backs it up: "Changing your posture, breathing, and rhythm can all change your brain, thereby reducing stress, depression, and anxiety, and leading to a feeling of well-being."

> “ *Move your body, change your mind.* ”
>
> *RACHEL HOLLIS*

## Get outside

Nature is so good for the soul. Being outside and breathing in the fresh air for a few minutes can give you a much-needed sense of calm and perspective if you are in a bad mood. Sitting and admiring a beautiful forest or lake can bring your focus onto something outside of your head, which is always needed when we are trying to solve a problem or make a decision.

How long is long enough to make an impact?

Research at Yale says 120 minutes a week. That's less than eighteen minutes a day.

No excuses—cut out one social-media scroll session a day and go for a walk instead. Even if you can't unplug from your tech, scroll on a park bench, or listen to a podcast while you walk. Your body and your mind will thank you.

> “ *Wilderness is not a luxury but a necessity of the human spirit.* ”
>
> EDWARD ABBEY

## *There's nothing quite like a snuggle with your favourite pet*

Having a connection to an animal has long been proven to improve your health and happiness. It doesn't even need to be YOUR animal—just being around animals can lower your stress hormone (cortisol) and increase your happiness hormone (oxytocin).

Go ahead and do your friend a favour and cat-sit while she's out of town. Take your pal's best canine friend for a spin around the block or visit your local farm or petting zoo to get your dose of feel-good.

> “*Animals are such agreeable friends—they ask no questions; they pass no criticisms.*”
>
> GEORGE ELIOT

# You are what you eat

You've heard it before. But have you noticed the truth of it in your own life yet?

I like to consider it through the lens of a computer programming phrase: Garbage in, garbage out.

This means if you are putting garbage into a system (in this case, your body) then you can expect garbage results to be produced. As true as this is for organizational systems and software, it is equally as true for the human body.

If you feed yourself junk, you are going to feel crappy. We all know this. But it feels too important (and simple) to ignore.

Drink water. Eat real food. Limit your sugar intake.

If this feels daunting, take it in small steps. Commit to drinking an extra glass of water every day for a week. The next week, switch out one snack a day for a non-processed version. You'll gain momentum when you start to feel the results. It's not about how you look or losing weight. It's about how you FEEL and improving your brain function and overall health.

*Affirmation:*
*I trust my body to tell me everything it needs.*

# *Change your thoughts*

Negative thoughts manifest into chemical reactions that can impact your body by bringing more stress into your system and decreasing your immunity.

Read that again.

**YOUR THOUGHTS CAN PHYSICALLY CHANGE YOUR BODY.**

Start becoming aware of the negative thoughts you have and be intentional about stopping them or, even better, flip the script to something positive instead.

*Did you know?*
*Anxiety and excitement are the same physical feeling in your body, it's the meaning you assign to the physical sensations that determines your experience. Next time you feel anxious tell your body and brain out loud that "I am excited."*

## Prioritize relaxation

It's so important for your body and your brain to have some time "off" to decompress and wander. Take a spa day, sleep in, watch a movie, or read a magazine. Catch up with your friends. Whatever it is that is relaxing for you, do more of that.

When? That's the tough part, isn't it? Start small and try to schedule thirty minutes a week of relaxation. When you look at your week at a glance, if you don't see relaxation scheduled, a red flag should go up.

*Tip:*

*Schedule a half hour each week to just be. Put it right there in your calendar and show up for this time like it's a non-negotiable appointment with yourself.*

## *Goal setting 101*

When you are making goals, health-related or otherwise, one of the most important things to do is to make sure your goal is attainable. Can you see yourself achieving it? It should feel like a stretch, but not a leap.

If you believe you can reach your goal, you are much more likely to stick with it through the hard work required to get there.

As you gain momentum through doing the steps to achieve your goal you will become more motivated – so celebrate your wins as you make progress!

*Affirmation:*
*I can do hard things.*

## Be your own advocate

If things don't feel right, say something. Too often we stay silent for fear of being wrong or judged, but it is vitally important to stand up for your health and well-being, and that of your family and loved ones.

If something feels off, it probably is. Be persistent and stand your ground when bringing concerns to your health practitioners. They are busy, they are overwhelmed, but you deserve to be heard and no one is going to come to your rescue, so it's on you to speak up.

*Affirmation:*
*I will be my own best advocate.*

## *Hustle culture is overrated*

Rest is important. Exercise is important. Eating well is important. Make time for these things.

*A quick mindfulness practice:*

*Lie down and get comfortable.*
*Take three deep breaths.*
*Starting at your toes, slowly bring your awareness to each part of your body and try to relax it as much as possible.*
*Move from your toes to your feet, your ankles, calves, all the way up to the top of your head.*
*This can take five or fifty minutes, whatever you have available and whatever feels right for you.*

## *You are not alone*

Mental health has become a hot topic in the last decade, and for good reason. It is of critical importance that we not only keep our bodies healthy and active but our minds also.

The stigma is still lingering, but if you are struggling, know that every person you connect with has either suffered, is suffering, or loves someone who is suffering from depression, anxiety, loneliness, eating disorders, mood swings, obsessive-compulsive disorder, social anxiety, etc. You're not alone. Nor are they.

We all need to do our part to realize we are interconnected and help one another, because life is hard enough without adding the pressure of feeling "less than."

*If you want to bring an instant spark to your day, here is a quick way to do it: Make someone else feel special.*

## *Did you know that insomnia isn't always physical?*

It is often a mental condition. This is good news because there is a lot you can do to help yourself if you suffer from it. Lack of sleep can cause many physical and mental problems, so it's important to tackle insomnia when it comes up.

Try waking up at the same time every single day, even on the weekends. Don't go to bed until you are ready to sleep, and if you are tossing and turning, don't just sit there counting sheep and getting stressed as the minutes tick on by. It is important to get out of bed and go do a quiet activity until you are sleepy again. You can train your brain to associate bed and sleep.

*One of my favourite ways to kick insomnia to the curb is to move the body. Shake your sillies out. Dance. It changes the chemistry of your body and snaps you out of your mental pattern.*

There are things you can do during the day also: practice mindfulness, meditation, and deep breathing techniques to help teach your body to relax. Remember that you have made it through hard days of being tired before, and you can do it again if you have a bad night. Take the pressure off.

## Stay above the line

Imagine a piece of paper with a horizontal line drawn through it that represents a benchmark. The benchmark can be for a goal, or simply how you want to feel. When you notice that you're operating below the line (i.e., not doing the things you said that you would, or not feeling the way you want to) you can start to make small, incremental shifts right in the moment to bring you back up to (or above) this line.

For example: If you have a goal to get healthy and halfway through the day you check in and realize you are below the line (perhaps you skipped your morning workout, or you couldn't resist the donuts at the office), you have two choices:

1. Throw in the towel and call the entire day a wash. Eat a cheeseburger and veg on the couch, or
2. Acknowledge where you are, have a glass of water, and go for a ten-minute walk.

It's not about being above the line all the time—that is impossible. It's about recognizing when you are below it and using that as an opportunity to recalibrate. James Clear, author of Atomic Habits, has this lovely view that with every decision you make, you are casting a vote for the type of person you want to be. With enough votes cast in any direction, you ultimately are embodying and being that type of person. A glass of water and a midday walk cast a vote towards you being a person who prioritizes their health.

*Either you control your attitude, or it controls you.*

# Mindfulness

We all know that living in the past is dumb. It's gone. And the future isn't here yet, so worrying or wishing for things that may or may not be is a waste of our energy. It only makes sense that focusing on the present moment is the smart thing to do.

So why don't we? Why is it so hard to simply stop and take in our surroundings, use all our senses to engage with the present moment?

An easy way you can start to be mindful is to set an alarm on your phone at pre-determined times throughout the day. The alarm will remind you to stop, take a deep breath, and look around. Good, bad, or otherwise, your present environment is all you have and if you can fully embrace where you are, you can work towards letting go of worries about the past or future and free up that mind space for your task at hand.

*Anchor yourself in the present moment:*
*Identify five things you can see, four things you can hear, three things you can feel, two things you can smell, and one thing you can taste. Or simply look for five things that are the colour blue. Focusing on what is in front of you is the point here.*

# Wealthy

I'm going to be a bit sneaky here, because when I talk about wealth it's not just about financial resources. It includes abundance in all areas of your life: career, relationships, family, friendships, joy, etc. Because the word "wealthy" fits perfectly into the title of the book, for the purpose of a good rhyme we are going with that as the chapter name.

In honesty, what I am bringing to you in this section is ideas, advice, and inspiration on how to live a wealthy, or abundant, life in many different areas. Yes, some of these pages will be filed with typical financial stuff. But you are also going to find super useful advice on how to create abundance in other areas of your life that we don't typically measure.

The best way that I know how to obtain abundance is through manifesting, by having an abundance mindset and remembering it every single day.

Manifesting isn't about magic. To me, manifesting is another word for creating. Two things are required: a goal and hard work. You must know where you are going and stay the course to get anything worthwhile in life.

Do we have the potential to have whatever life we want? Absolutely. Within reason, and with the hands we were dealt. Overall, as a sweeping generalization, there is absolutely nothing holding you back from the life you desire except yourself. Flip through these pages to get inspired and learn the tips and tricks that will help you get started on your manifesting journey to overall abundance, as well as some tried and true financial tips for your very real spending and saving habits.

*Are you ready to manifest the life of your dreams? Come check out* ***jillwright.ca/ freebies*** *for free resources to get you started, including meditations, EFT tapping sessions, affirmations, workshop replays, book and podcast recommendations and more!*

## *Pay in cash*

Be realistic and aware of your financial situation and spend only what you have, so when you're out of money, you are out of money. Credit is quicksand and once you get in, it can be SO hard to get out of it.

Go to the bank on payday and get $20 bills. Separate it into envelopes with the amount of money you have pre-budgeted to each expense category (gas, food, entertainment, etc.). I understand that we are in a digital world and bills are paid online, so try this technique with your disposable income only at first.

Seeing money physically disappear has a WAY bigger impact on your respect for your money than simply swiping or tapping a card does.

Racking up debt in the form of interest and spending on credit is detrimental to your financial dignity. It can seem harmless in the moment to pull out your credit card to pay for gas, but if you don't pay off your card each month, things can start to accumulate fast.

If I could go back to my 16-year-old self and give her ONE piece of advice, this is what it would be: Live within your means.

*Debt is like quicksand.*

## *Appreciate what you have*

My Grandpa's favourite quote, the one that stuck with my Mom the most, was, "Don't try to keep up with the Joneses, because the Joneses will just move on you."

She took this to mean that you should be happy with what you have, rather than always trying to get the bigger, better, newer thing just because your neighbours or friends or colleagues have it.

This is such timeless and practical advice. If we are always saying "we will be happy when..." then we are by definition always chasing something, and never able to appreciate and enjoy what we have in this moment. Chances are, what you have right now, in this very moment, is enough.

Cultivate an abundance mindset: there is plenty out there for everybody.

This is the opposite of a scarcity mindset, in which we operate out of a place of lack.

> "*The opposite of scarcity is not abundance; the opposite of scarcity is simply enough.*"
>
> *BRENÉ BROWN*

## *Break it into chunks*

My Dad always taught me to break problems or projects into small pieces. Focusing on only one step at a time can help overwhelming tasks seem less scary to get through, and each time you accomplish one thing on the list it is cause for celebration, making you feel more committed and motivated to achieving the thing.

*Affirmation:*
*Done is better than perfect.*

## *Save Mama Earth and your wallet*

Consign your items and shop second-hand! Instead of throwing things out, if they are in good condition when you are done with them, bring them to your local consignment store and try to sell them. Not only will you be avoiding adding to the landfills, but you will earn some sweet green when your items sell to their next owner.

On the flip side, we don't need to be buying everything new. This is especially true for things like kids' clothing, toys, and books, which they grow out of so quickly. Books for adults too, now that I think of it.

> “ *The key to abundance is meeting limited circumstances with unlimited thoughts.* ”
>
> *MARIANNE WILLIAMSON*

## *Treat yourself (once in a while)*

There is no joy in constantly scrimping and saving. The results and the rewards of saving are long term, so it's important to celebrate your good habits and treat yourself every now and again to stay motivated.

This will reaffirm the good intention behind saving and watching your spending and give you motivation to keep doing it.

*Affirmation:*
*Abundance is my birthright.*

## *Stay the course*

Consistency is Queen. Keep doing the things that are going to bring you closer to your personal best. Be consistent and see your efforts produce the results you are looking for.

Patience is required; in fact, it's the price of admission to your abundant life.

Show up and be consistent with your efforts. Keep showing up. Keep learning. Even on the days you don't feel like it. Be willing to do the things other people aren't willing to do. Keep going past the point where other people stop. Your success comes after you face your biggest obstacle.

> “*When you are grateful, fear disappears, and abundance appears.*”
>
> *TONY ROBBINS*

## *Use your creativity and get resourceful*

There is often a cheaper, better, or faster way to do something if you just stop and think it over from a fresh perspective.

Bring in a trusted friend, colleague, or family member and hash out different ways to overcome a challenge you are facing. Chances are when you step back and let go of your attachment to the process, you will come up with a completely different angle that will get you to your desired result in a more aligned way.

> “ *When you want something, all the universe conspires in helping you to achieve it.* ”
>
> *PAULO COELHO*

## *Stretch your money as far as you can*

Buy in bulk when you can to take advantage of economies of scale. Buy used instead of new or borrow/swap with someone—the barter system is not dead! Check out your local flea markets, thrift and consignment stores, and dollar stores for great deals on things you need, so you can save some money to treat yourself to the things you want every now and again.

> “*Abundance is not something we acquire; it is something we tune into.*”
>
> *DR. WAYNE W. DYER*

## *Habits pay dividends*

Saving is important, but the habit of doing it is more important than the amount you put away.

Start with a weekly goal of $5. Open an account (or a mason jar) and commit to putting aside $5 a week from now until forever.

Once you have a few weeks of accomplishing this under your belt, you will start to identify as someone who saves money each week. You will start to change your self-identity in this way because you will see the proof.

Once you start to believe that you are, in fact, someone who can save money, everything changes.

Another way to get started is to put aside $1 this week. Literally, into an old coffee can or a mason jar. Next week, add $2. Keep contributing by adding an additional $1 weekly, and by the time a year has passed you will have put away $1,378 without ever putting aside more than $52 a week.

> “ *There are only two ways to live your life. One is as though nothing is a miracle. The other is as though everything is a miracle.* ”
>
> ALBERT EINSTEIN

# Manifesting 101

Manifesting is a beautiful tool, and the first step is knowing with crystal clarity what you want to manifest.

Ask. Believe. Receive. Set an intention for what it is that you want to attract or create, believe it is already yours, and surrender control of the how to the universe.

Imagine the goal vividly in your mind. Set tangible milestones to get there. Feel what it will be like to accomplish that goal. What your life will be life. How you will feel. What that will mean for you.

When you have that emotional connection and clarity attached to your goal it makes working toward it so much easier. You are also raising your vibration by feeling the positive emotions in advance, which allows the universe to align your goal with you and bring you opportunities.

Your dreams will manifest when the time is right, but you can move things along by being crystal clear on what you want, directly asking for it, and letting go of controlling exactly how it will occur.

*Affirmation:*
*There is NO LIMIT to what I can attract into my life.*

## *Pay yourself first*

Set aside a portion of your paycheck to go towards an income opportunity for your future. Whether it is contributing to a retirement plan or an investment portfolio, or starting an emergency fund, make sure you are setting aside at least 2% of your take-home pay (after taxes have been taken off).

When you start off that is likely to be somewhere between $20 and $40 a paycheck. Totally doable, right? It isn't going to make you a millionaire in five years, but it is going to be a start and it will set you up with the right habits to expand your contributions as your financial situation evolves.

> “*Be thankful for what you have; you'll end up having more. If you concentrate on what you don't have, you will never, ever have enough.*”

*OPRAH WINFREY*

## *Make the library your best friend*

There are thousands of books available for you to read, for FREE. Along this same vein, find your other bookworm friends and start a book swap. Your community might even have a local lending library run by a neighbour.

You don't need to buy books new, even if you live in a smaller community without these resources–check online. Used books are so much less expensive and you can even sell them again when you are done with them. Win-win!

*Thought:*
*The happiest of people don't necessarily have the best of everything; they just make the most of everything.*

## *Have you ever considered a dinner club?*

Grab a few of your best friends or favorite couples and take turns hosting the group at each other's house for dinner, rather than going out to eat. It lends an air of friendly competition, intimacy, and, best of all, saves you the money otherwise spent on dining at a restaurant.

> "*See yourself living in abundance and you will attract it. It always works; it works every time with every person.*"
>
> BOB PROCTOR

## Get crafty

If you're someone who marks occasions like birthdays with a card, why not get creative and try your hand at making a card instead of buying one?

Same goes for gifts themselves. Pinterest is your best friend here, but a few ideas could be cookies, jam, placemats, picture frames, homemade lotions and potions, scrapbooks, a recipe book, etc.

> “ *Acknowledging the good that you already have in your life is the foundation for all abundance.* ”
>
> ECKHART TOLLE

## Get educated

Take control of your finances by learning the basics about money, budgeting, investing, etc. You don't need a bunch of savings to get going.

Read a book.

Find some teachers and mentors on Instagram and follow along, sign up for their freebies, and put all that valuable (and free) information into practice.

Google and YouTube can be your best friends in your search for financial education resources.

*Affirmation:*
*I am worthy of everything in abundance.*

## *Assume that people are operating with good intentions*

Even if the wording is wrong, the suggestion or advice unwelcome, or the outcome inconvenient, people generally don't go around wanting to make life miserable for one another.

We usually operate with cooperation and helpfulness in mind and though it might not be received that way by you, it probably was intended with love, kindness, or consideration. Change your mindset and start to believe in an abundance of kindness around you.

> "*The fastest way to bring more wonderful examples of abundance into your personal experience is to take constant notice of the wonderful things that are already there.*"
>
> *ESTHER HICKS*

## *Replay your day*

Before you close your eyes at night, go back through your day and replay the positive moments, the feelings of love. FEEL into them again, as if they were happening right that moment. Anchor the feeling of gratitude for those moments into your heart.

> "*Gratitude is one of the strongest and most transformative states of being. It shifts your perspective from lack to abundance and allows you to focus on the good in your life, which in turn pulls more goodness into your reality.*"
>
> JEN SINCERO

## *Back that ass up*

Everyone should have a "back your ass up" file, at work and for life in general. This is an email folder or a paper folder where you keep all the important documents you need to prove something if it ever comes into question.

Receipts, emails, letters—even just a handwritten note by you, dated, noting down what was said or done so you don't forget. It's a place to keep a trail of information.

Since it is all in one place, you will know where to go if you need to back your ass up.

## *Money is a lousy way of keeping score*

Focus instead on the other areas of your life where you feel abundant: your career, your relationships, your education, etc. There are so many other measuring sticks to judge yourself against than simply the financial side.

*Reframe:*
*What are all the ways you get paid? In compliments, in kindness, in smiles, in hugs, in testimonials, etc.? Focus on these instead of just cash.*

## *Personal development is all about showing up*

There is no easy button to getting where we want in life, to achieving the status, the success, or the accolades you so want so badly. You have to show up and you have to do the work.

PS–it's worth it!

*Affirmation:*
*My compelling future is my lighthouse to guide me.*

## *Investing in yourself yields dividends well into the future*

By far, the best investment you can make is in yourself. If you have a dream or a goal, and you have the will and determination to make it happen, investing in education, courses, conferences, and/or books is a great way to get started.

When you invest in yourself, you are telling your subconscious you are worth it. Your dream is worth it. You will work harder to make it a reality for yourself as a result. An investment in your own skill set has never-ending dividends and payback.

Consider your return on time as well as your return on investment. Think of the time you are getting back by learning and developing new skills so that you can be more efficient. The time you save by discovering the path that is right for you instead of wasting more years going down an unfulfilling life path. Think of the shift in energy you get by aligning your life with your dreams and goals. Self-investment is always about more than just the money.

*The most important resources are time, money, and energy. You need to invest all three to make it to where you want to go. It's not always all about the green.*

## *The 80/20 Rule*

The Pareto principle, also known as the 80/20 rule, is a theory maintaining that 80% of the output from a given situation or system is determined by 20% of the input.

20% of your customers will give you 80% of your revenue.

20% of the exercises you do at the gym will give you 80% of your muscle.

Think about how this applies in your own life: you probably spend 80% of your social time with 20% of your friend group. 20% of your social media posts probably have 80% of the engagement on your account.

You want to live in this 20% zone. Why spend extra time or energy on things that aren't producing additional results?

You don't need to put in 100% effort to get results; 20% is more than enough as long as it is the right activity.

*Affirmation:*
*I commit to living in my zone of genius, now and forever.*

## *Motivation and inspiration don't create transformation*

Transformation comes through the transaction. You need to invest in believing in yourself.

Hire that personal trainer to keep you accountable to your health goals.

Join the online program to learn how to self-publish your book.

Hire a coach or go to therapy to do the work to find alignment with yourself.

You must pay to play, because if you pay, you pay attention.

*What is the cost of your inaction? Sometimes the opportunity cost of NOT acting on an opportunity far outweighs the cost of the education/experience itself.*

## *Kaizen*

Kaizen is a Japanese word that describes the idea of continuous growth through small, consistent changes that reap significant improvements over time.

Take things one step at a time. Small, manageable chunks. You just have to start. Remember that small hinges swing a big door.

If you shift the trajectory of your life even one degree in a different direction your destination will look completely different in a year, five years, or ten years.

“ *You can choose courage, or you can choose comfort, but you cannot choose both.* ”

*BRENÉ BROWN*

## *Manage your mindset*

Your mindset is what will ultimately allow you to take the action needed to make real change in your life.

Change your thoughts, change your self-talk, change your life. Our thoughts manifest into our reality, so take care to really cultivate a nurturing and positive mindset.

*Affirmation:*
*I can afford to buy anything I want.*

# Wise

The Cambridge Dictionary defines wise as "having or showing the ability to make good judgments, based on a deep understanding and experience of life."

Dictionary.com states that the primary difference between the knowledge and wisdom is that "wisdom involves a healthy dose of perspective and the ability to make sound judgments about a subject while knowledge is simply knowing."

What do I mean when I write about being wise? Being aware, being intentional, being connected to your soul and inner knowing. Using resources and tools to create a life you want. Knowing how to connect with yourself and others in a way that results in the highest good for all.

Wisdom is an accumulation of knowledge based on experience, that you can use to help you make decisions and create the life you want.

Isn't that what we're all after?

Intuition is an inner knowingness. We all possess it, but many of us have buried it, stopped listening to it, and relinquished our power to the outside world. We look externally for answers, for clarity, for certainty, and for permission. We've turned it around backwards and inside out.

Stop searching for meaning externally. It must come from within. The only truth is from your soul. Not what other people say, think, or feel. Not what society or media tells us. Your intuition is a sacred tool that is always available. It takes practice to see it, feel it, and remember how to trust it.

Start by noticing when you feel goosebumps out of the blue. What's happening? Is it a situation you know is wrong? Or is it something that is so true and so right? Everyone's body gives them different signs. Did you have a headache appear from nowhere? Who are you with? Where are you? What is happening around you? Is this your body's way of telling you that you need a break from the situation, that it isn't serving you?

Trust your gut instincts. Feel into people's hearts. Follow your random thoughts. All these things are your intuition trying to get your attention and guide you. Start tuning in and the frequency will get louder and louder.

Pema Chödrön, a Buddhist nun, talks about the concept of shenpa, which is the very real human action of getting sucked into harmful coping mechanisms like drinking, shopping, judging, or even putting up proverbial walls in an attempt to escape our negative emotions or deal with discomfort. We do this all the time, and once we get "hooked" on doing this, it is difficult for us to change our behaviour. Our reaction becomes a habit, and we don't even know we are doing it, or why.

How do we stop getting hooked into behaviour to try to avoid emotions like shame, blame, fear, and jealousy, when it feels so involuntary in the first place? The answer is to actually feel them. Feel the "bad" emotions.

When we feel an uncomfortable situation coming on, one we normally would run from or try to numb, we should instead shake it up before it gets its hooks into us, and we go down the old familiar road. See if you can simply notice the discomfort and acknowledge it without engaging with it. Instead of turning to your habitual reaction, come back to the present moment. Just break the chain, bit by bit.

Research by neuroscientist Rick Hanson shows that 15 seconds is all you need. Even if you end up giving into your old habit, when you spend 15 seconds simply acknowledging the feeling before engaging in the old coping mechanism you are starting to re-wire your brain. The existing neural pathways are weakened by the 15 second gap between the trigger and the reaction.

> *It takes fifteen seconds of courage to change your life.*
>
> COLLEEN HOOVER

It takes practice, but if you can learn to feel the discomfort of life and detach yourself from your learned reaction, you achieve true wisdom and clarity. The discomfort in life isn't going anywhere, but if you can relax into it and refrain from reacting, you will gain immense perspective.

This section of the book is designed to give you insights on how to use your wisdom and inner knowing, and to provide you with the tools and resources you perhaps didn't know yet that can support you in your journey to living wisely. On being productive and goal focused.

I hope you enjoy these ideas, tips and motivations and use them to live the inspired life that you truly deserve.

> *The journey of a thousand miles begins with one step.*
>
> LAO TZU

*Add some wisdom to your personal toolbox. Check out* ***jillwright.ca/freebies*** *for free resources including meditations, EFT tapping sessions, affirmations, workshops, book and podcast recommendations and more!*

## *Eat your frog*

That phrase comes from a story that says if the first thing you do each morning is eat a live frog, nothing worse can happen for the rest of the day. Productivity guru Brian Tracy says that your frog should be the most difficult thing on your to-do list. That thing you are most likely to procrastinate on. Because if you eat that frog first, it's gonna give you energy and momentum for the rest of the day.

If you leave the frog there, staring at you all day, and you work on a hundred other unimportant things, it's gonna drain your energy because sure, you might be crossing things off the list, but your mind is never far from that disgusting frog taking up space on your desk and in your brain.

So do the most important thing first. Don't give yourself the chance to put it off. You're going to be truly amazed at how quickly the needle starts to move on achieving your goals.

*It isn't being perfect that makes the difference. It is simply committing to showing up in a way that you can sustain and feel good about.*

*Be selfish with your time in the short term so you can be the best version of yourself in the long term*

Taking time to rest and do what YOU want to do is imperative to keeping you grounded and centered.

If you aren't grounded and centered, you aren't going to show up as the best version of yourself. Which impacts everyone around you.

Be selfish so that you can be a better partner, friend, parent, or coworker.

*Who is steering your ship? You should be the author of your own life, the designer of your own destiny, the captain of your own ship.*

## *Use your intuition*

It's your inner compass and the way your higher self/soul/subconscious communicates with you. It's there to keep you safe, and to lead you to the things that will serve your highest good.

Because this voice is your inner truth, it doesn't feel like it needs to prove itself. That's why it can be so quiet. In order to really hear it you need to practice getting quiet. Listen. Turn in. Let that little voice speak up!

*Tip:*
*Stop taking advice from people who don't have the life you want.*

## *Make your day better by making someone else's day better*

Pay someone a compliment, hold the door, send a wink, whatever you can do that is authentic and kind.

Do that and make your day better by making someone else's day better.

Seriously. The look you get from them is better than any caffeine boost.

Some people are annoying, clingy, and make you irritable or crazy—but perhaps they are just lonely and looking for an outlet to connect to another human being, or a friendly smile or a shared experience.

Everyone needs someone and while you don't have to be every person's sounding board, you can make a difference in someone's life just by offering kindness or a few moments of your attention.

> "*You can tell more about a person by what he says about others than you can by what others say about him.*"

AUDREY HEPBURN

# *Live and let live*

Honestly, just mind your own business. You do you, be authentically YOU, and let other people be authentically them.

At the end of the day, their life choices are none of your business anyway, so why waste your time, energy, and emotions on things you can't change and that don't affect you?

The only person you can control is yourself, and the only person who can control you is you.

*Don't worry about things that are out of your control. Fix the things that ARE in your control.*

## *You can only do the best you can with what you have at the time*

This includes knowledge, resources, time, energy, etc. You can't get blood from a stone, they say, and likewise, you can't exceed your present circumstance.

That's not to say you can't advance. You just need to accept that at each step along the journey, your abilities and successes will look different based on where you are in that journey, what you've learned, and whether you keep applying it and growing or not. That is what will determine whether your best improves or remains stagnant. After all, as the great Maya Angelou famously said, "when you know better, you do better."

Success leaves clues. Find someone who is doing what you want to be doing and doing it better than you. Learn from them!

*learn·ing /'lər-niŋ: Trying, failing, making bad decisions, changing your mind, and GROWING FROM IT.*

*You cannot change the people*
*around you, but you can change*
*the people around you*

*Read that again.*

## *You are responsible for your own destiny*

Only YOU can make changes to your life. If you're not changing your life, you are choosing your life.

Take risks, take chances. Be bold and be yourself. AS humans we are so afraid to fail, to lose, to hurt, or to look silly that we don't even try. If you never try, you will never know.

Sure, things might go badly. They might not (make that WILL not) go perfectly. Isn't your dream worth the chance? Because ... what if it works?

*It is never going to be perfect. Replace "it" with anything, and the statement holds.*

## *Know when to let it go, when to make a change, and when to fight*

When you are facing a decision or a fork in the road, there are always three options: move on, adjust/adapt, or go all in.

Sit quietly with yourself and listen to what your soul has to say.

Is this a moment to release? Or to pour your heart into it? Maybe it's neither and there is a balance to be had somewhere in the middle.

Figure out what serves your highest good and take direct action in alignment with that decision. Trust your instinct on this.

*Imagine you have unlimited support. What things in your life do you simply want to let go?*

## *Everyone has a different reality*

We all live here on Earth together, but we each experience life in a unique personal way that is not and cannot be the same as the way other people experience it.

Understand that your reality, your understanding of a situation, is based on your personal lens. Those around you, even your siblings, partner, best friend, and parents all have a different pair of glasses on. So yes, stand in your truth, but also be gracious and accept that your truth isn't THE truth.

If we have an uncomfortable interaction with someone, whether in person or online, it can be easy to judge or feel resentment or hurt, anger, jealousy, etc. Remember that those are YOUR emotions, not the other person's. You never know where that person is coming from, what they are thinking or feeling, or how they are interpreting the same situation or conversation.

Everyone has their own story, and it impacts how they show up and how they react to life. Two people can look at the exact same thing and see something totally different.

*Everyone has a story. Don't assume you know what it is.*

*If you feel like you don't have time, what is actually happening is that you don't have clarity*

We all have the same amount of time: 24 hours in a day. How we prioritize it and spend it is based on what is important to us, our goals, and our values (and our resources, but that is a whole other conversation).

My point is that if you find yourself saying you don't have time for something, figure out if that thing is important to you or not. Figure out where you want to go in your life, and why.

Then shift the way you manage your time to accommodate the things you are striving to achieve and eliminate the things you don't care about. Schedule in the things that are "needle movers" to accomplishing your goals. Schedule in your "me time". Schedule in the family connection time. Align your life with your values and you will experience immense time freedom!

*Affirmation:*
*Time isn't something I find; it is something I make.*

## The Emotional Bank Account

With every relationship you have in your life, there exists an invisible force which Stephen Covey calls the Emotional Bank Account (EBA for short).

The idea is that every positive interaction, every nice thing you do for someone, every compliment, every time you show someone you have their back, whatever it is—every positive thing is a deposit into the EBA with that person. The same is true of that person towards you. You are joint cardholders.

Eventually, you are going to have a bad day. You are going to need something from that person. You are going to need to make a withdrawal in time, energy, or emotions. If your EBA balance is high, withdrawals don't rock the boat. You both know the ebb and flow and don't worry about the balance fluctuating now and again. You're invested for the long term.

The trouble is when you fail to make deposits, or if one person is continually depositing and the other continually withdrawing. If the EBA balance is low between you, then any withdrawal, no matter how small, can seriously jeopardize the relationship because now you are in overdraft with that person, which is not sustainable.

> “ *When people show you who they really are – believe them.* ”
>
> MAYA ANGELOU

## *Write things down*

No one can remember everything and if you want to get something done or remember something important, write it down!

Use calendar reminders for birthdays and use a paper or digital planner for yoga classes or to schedule your dog's next vet appointment.

Then you can stop worrying about trying to remember it, and free your mind for other things.

*Tip:*
*If a task is gonna take five minutes or less, DO IT NOW. Don't add it to an ever-growing to-do list.*

## *Fear of failure comes with trying something new*

There's the fear of failure that comes with trying something new. The fear of looking silly when you are a beginner at something. The fear of starting small compared to other people. There are so many obstacles we face just in the decision to start working on ourselves. We often quit before we even get started because the road feels too long and hard to get from where we are now to where we want to be.

**What if you just went for it?**

What if, just this once, you decided to put on blinders to what anyone else might think, say, or feel about your decision? What if you could hold on to the conviction that this IS possible for you, and that you CAN achieve it? What if you gave yourself space to think of the future version of you? What you'll feel like when you reach your goal. How different your life will be. The pride you'll have in your success, knowing that you put in the work, and you DID IT. Whatever that is for you.

Now, imagine that you don't make a change. Imagine where your life will be in one, three, or five years. Imagine the missed opportunities. Is it worth robbing yourself of your full potential, of your dream future, just because you're scared to start small or scared of what other people might say?

> “ *Your next level lives on the other side of the thing you fear most.* ”
>
> *DEAN GRAZIOSI*

## Ask. For. Help.

Seriously. The only way I can "get it all done" is because I don't actually do it all myself. And I feel absolutely ZERO guilt about this. I'll tell you why.

I've learned that you can't have it all, but you can have what you want. To have the things you want, you need to prioritize what your wants are. Everything else is secondary. Focus your limited energy on the things that matter most to you and delegate the rest. Or ditch them.

Energy is a precious resource. Along with time and sleep, it is right up there as paramount for a successfully functioning human.

Be stingy with your energy. Focus it on the things that move you closer to the life you want.

## *Give your best to the ones you love the most*

It can be tempting to come home at the end of the day, tired from giving your all at work and being nice to everyone and drop your game face to just be you. If being yourself means retreating into your shell, or dumping on your partner about a bad day, or losing your patience with your kids, or simply curling up in bed because you are too tired to put the energy into conversation, then stop and evaluate.

Why did the strangers, the outsiders in your day, get your best, and the ones who love and support you at home get what's left? We so often get this backwards. Home, in the company of those who love you the most, is where we should be placing our patience, our positivity, our loving energy.

*Question:*
*What do others look for from you? Strength? Kindness? Laughter? Inspiration? Guidance? Love?*

## *Don't take things personally*

Did someone call you out at work or make a joke at your expense? I can almost guarantee their negativity or rudeness has more to do with what is going on with them in their life than it does with you.

Everyone has hurts and burdens. You can't know what is going on with someone else and how that is impacting their ability to empathize or be conscious of how they are appearing to others.

You don't know their internal struggles or what life is like for them. Everyone is dealing with their own issues, situations, emotions, and challenges.

*Give everyone some grace today. Even if that person is yourself.*

## *One coin, two sides*

Someone else's view might not match yours, but that doesn't mean they are wrong (or that you are wrong).

You can view things differently and still both be right.

Each person's personal beliefs and views are their own and don't impact you, so even if they differ, they are true for that person in their current circumstances based on their history and experience. The same way that your views are for you.

*Our background and circumstances may have influenced who we are, but we are responsible for who we become.*

## *Instincts can be wrong (gasp!)*

Though it goes against most of the advice I give to trust your intuition, you don't have to automatically go with your gut. If your first reaction feels like it is based on anger, stress, or fear, try not to take it at face value.

Maybe it's based on your mood at that moment; maybe you are short on time and it's the easy way; maybe it doesn't actually solve the problem.

Take a step back and find a creative solution to your problem. Bring others into the mix. Consider the big picture and find a solution that is the most beneficial to all parties involved. When you are in a calmer headspace and have considered your options, then it's time to trust your instincts.

*A decision made from fear is usually the wrong decision.*

## *Friendship*

No matter how good a friend is, they're going to hurt you every once in a while, and you can forgive them for that.

*We don't have to change friends if we understand that friends change.*

## *Living with intention*

Living intentionally means you're constantly aware of, and planning for, how you'll show up in every area of your life. When you focus on how you want to show up it forces you to be present and mindful.

So how do you live with intention? What does it look like in action?

Think about the things you want to do in each area of your life (family, career, health, social, relationships, finances, etc.) and plan how you need to show up in those areas to move you closer to your goal.

Focus on being present to ensure you are living up to your own intentions for that situation. The trick is to focus in advance on the outcome you want to achieve. It really helps to visualize it too. Maybe that's taking things a bit too far for you. But hey, all the pro athletes do it, so it's good enough for me.

*Affirmation:*
*I am expanding in abundance, success, and love every single day.*

## Get ahead of the game

Choose your outfits for the entire week on Sunday night. Bonus points if you have pieces that can be mixed and matched.

Set out the week's wardrobe somewhere you can see it each morning and it will save you tons of time choosing an outfit because you've already thoughtfully narrowed down your options.

Happily, this gets even easier as the week goes on and you have fewer things to choose from!

*Do it right the first time; it's faster and more efficient than having to do it again. Best practice is to only touch something once.*

## *Put a timer on your social media use*

I know this one seems like a no-brainer, but you need to honestly give it a try. Having specific time set aside for social media means you can focus on your responsibilities when you need to without distraction, and you can be fully present in your social media scroll when you are intentionally taking time for that.

Consider adding social media as an actual appointment in your calendar. The trick is giving yourself a set time to take the social media break so that you aren't always yearning for it while you are trying to get actual work done, and you can scroll guilt free when it's designated social media time.

> “*Convenience and commitment don't live on the same block.*”
>
> *LISA NICHOLS*

## *The Biggest Lie...*

I want to take a moment and call out one of the biggest lies we have all been told and believe: that multitasking is a good way to get more done.

For goodness's sake, do NOT multitask.

Focus your attention on one thing at a time, get it done, and move on. You'll be infinitely more productive if you allow yourself to focus on one thing a time instead of bouncing back and forth between tasks.

It takes a surprising amount of mental energy to switch your focus mid-task and then switch back again. Studies have shown that if our brain must constantly shift gears and bounce back and forth between tasks, we become less efficient and more likely to make a mistake. So be smart and stay focused. You'll cross things off your to-do list way faster, which could serve as fuel to keep the momentum going.

> "*There's nothing so fatiguing as the eternal hanging on of an uncompleted task.*"
>
> *WILLIAM JAMES*

## *A quick reframe can change everything*

The next time you find yourself saying, "I don't have time for that," rephrase it and say out loud, "That isn't important to me" and see how that makes you feel.

GAME CHANGER.

Instead of saying, "I don't have time to work out," say, "Moving my body and getting healthy isn't important to me." How does that feel?

Or instead of, "I don't have time to play with the kids," try, "Having a connection with my kids isn't important to me." Ouch.

Or maybe even instead of, "I don't have time to do all of the housework," try, "Having a clean home isn't important to me at this stage of my life."

Knowing when something isn't important can help you ditch the guilt about not doing that thing.

> " *If you don't like something, change it. If you can't change it, change your attitude.* "

*MAYA ANGELOU*

# Action trumps all

We are in control of the effort we put in and therefore the results we see. You have to work for it.

Ninety percent of the success that the world sees as "overnight" is hard work put in during the times no one is watching.

Ed Sheeran busked on the streets of London and self-released his music before he was ever "discovered".

EL James was turned down by two literary agents before Fifty Shades of Grey became a worldwide sensation.

Mark Ruffalo went to 600 casting auditions that amounted to nothing before he landed a major acting role.

Success is inevitable when you take the right action and show up consistently. You are rewarded in public for what you practice in private and are willing to risk in public.

*If you aren't failing, you aren't learning. What did you fail at today?*

## *Don't settle*

To achieve the result you want, you must see it, feel it, and believe it.

Get clear.

Know your why, the reason behind your goal. Focus on your result—how that will feel, and what your life will look like when you achieve your goal.

Write it down every day in a journal. Put your goals on paper and write how you will feel when you achieve them.

Say no to anything else.

*Affirmation:*
*I have a vision for my life, and I am not willing to settle for anything less.*

## *Whom you surround yourself with matters*

Learn from people who have achieved the thing you want. Who have the life you want.

If you can get around people in person who do the thing you want to do that is wonderful, but not everyone has access to the types of mentors and success stories we want to emanate.

Listen to podcasts. Get in Facebook groups. Go on a news diet and monitor the content you are taking in. Cut out toxic people. Read books. Go on YouTube. Watch TED talks.

Find your people and fill our world with them, immerse yourself in their world and watch what happens to yours.

> “ *You're the average of the five people you spend the most time with.* ”
>
> JIM ROHN

## *Habits are everything*

You are going to need next-level capabilities, habits, and resources to get to your next level. You need to bump bad habits out of your life so you can make room for new ones.

Set your intention. Make a morning or night routine and include things that will help keep you focused: journaling, gratitude, meditation, goal setting, etc.

According to James Clear, on average, it takes more than 2 months before a new behavior becomes automatic — 66 days to be exact.

Start today. It's ok to miss one day, but don't miss two in a row.

*What result do you want?*
*Why do you want it?*
*What are you going to do to get it?*

## *You are going to fail*

Taking chances, starting something new, and working towards anything means you will fail. It's not if; it's when.

It is vital to really be prepared for that and keep showing up anyway.

There will be days when you fail. That's expected. That's required. Keep showing up and do your best.

Don't compare yourself to anyone else. Compare yourself to the version of you last week, last year, the last time you tried this thing.

*Be willing to be wrong. If you are always right, you can't possibly grow.*

*Every single activity is either moving you closer to or further from your goals*

It sounds harsh, but it really is helpful to think in this black-and-white way. Decide right now not to waste any more of your precious time on anything that isn't moving you closer to the life you want.

When you make this a nonnegotiable practice, you can ditch any feelings of guilt that come up. Why would you waste time feeling guilty about not prioritizing something that isn't important to you or isn't moving you closer to your ideal life?

Focus your energy on the things that matter most to you and say no to the rest. If it doesn't serve your goal, it doesn't deserve your time. Period.

The transformation of what you want comes in the application of what you are learning. Take uncomfortable action towards progress.

*Don't wait to be ready. You will never be ready.*

## *Empty you head*

A brain dump is simply writing down on paper all the ideas, thoughts, and questions swirling around your head.

Maybe the moment you close your eyes to get some much-needed rest, your brain goes into overdrive and shoves into your consciousness all of things you need to do. Then your mind is racing, and sleep is elusive.

Be prepared! Keep a pen and paper beside your bed. Write down all the random thoughts as they come, and then rest, knowing you can come back to the list in the morning when you're fresh.

The awesomeness of a brain dump is twofold:

1) you clear up mental space for creativity, and
2) because you've written it all down, you aren't likely to forget to handle something important

> “ *Once you have clarity, you can move mountains.* ”
>
> UNKNOWN

## *Calling all list-aholics*

As a self-proclaimed "list-aholic," I often get so wrapped up in the list-making itself that nothing ever gets crossed off. Can you relate to that? Thought so.

Rachel Hollis gave me the idea to create an "action" or "results" list, instead of a to-do list. Keep it short and sweet and only include the top three things you need to accomplish that day. Your frog, and a maximum of two others. The top things that, if they get done, you will know you moved the needle in the right direction.

Once those things are done, you can go in the million directions your brain wants to take you and use the rest of your day for creative or spontaneous tasks that tend to pop up.

I often find that if I allow myself the quiet, unscheduled space available once my big tasks are completed, I can be supercharged with creativity, and I actually have the time to be able to act on my new ideas!

*Perfection is the lowest standard on Earth. Why? Because it is impossible. It's an excuse.*

## Energy lists

Create three to-do lists for your day:

1. for a high-energy day,
2. for a medium-energy day, and
3. for a low-energy day

You can choose your daily to-do list based on how you are feeling, and if you have a day when you aren't feeling your best, you can still accomplish everything on your low-energy list and not have any guilt that you didn't get enough done.

Your low-energy list might just have "take out the garbage." Your medium-energy list could add on "fold the laundry" and your high-energy list may include garbage, laundry, and meal prep.

Brilliant, right?

*Are you busy? Of course, we all are! But are you productive? Does your activity create a result for you?*

## *Batch working 101*

A super helpful time-management trick I use a lot is batch working. The idea here is to lump all your similar tasks together and then do them all at once. Maybe on Mondays you do all your administrative work for your business; Tuesdays, you do your sales calls; Wednesday is your creative day when you focus just on content creation; Thursdays, you tackle household chores; you get the idea.

This way, your brain doesn't have to constantly shift focus from one thing to another, which saves you precious mental clarity and time. It's amazing how much energy we waste zigzagging from one thing to the next because our brain can't catch up as quickly as we think it does. It takes a minute to reacclimate to the first task once your attention has been taken away, which is the exact reason that multitasking is super inefficient.

*Knowledge is not power; knowledge is potential power. Power comes from action.*

## *Time Confetti*

I heard Ashley V. Whillans, an assistant professor at Harvard Business School, interviewed on a podcast and she was talking about a completely life-changing concept that I adopted immediately and still use daily.

What is it? The idea of time confetti. Sounds fun, right? It kinda is.

The idea is that we do have free time in our days, and quite a lot of it compared to past generations. This is in part thanks to modern inventions like the washing machine and the ATM. The problem is that our free time is split up into small portions throughout the day. Brief time slots when we are waiting in lines, commuting, and even waiting on hold.

What if we were intentional about using these brief moments of time? If we could fit small things into these pockets of time they could add up to big results. I liked the idea so much that created a time confetti list on my phone, which I look at every time I realize I have a few minutes available. I encourage you to do the same.

With a bit of practice, you'll soon start to pick up on these very frequent moments throughout the day and having a list to reference to help you use them wisely is just a super-smart and intentional thing to do!

# Nighttime Routines

Every single successful person that I know of has a morning routine. I hear them talk about it nonstop. Usually, it involves waking up before the kids to fit in a workout, journaling time, and gratitude work, followed by a quiet breakfast alone and making a to-do list for the day.

I get so discouraged and overwhelmed when I hear about it, because my kids wake up at the crack of dawn. I'm talking 4:30 a.m. Which should absolutely be illegal.

If you're a hardworking mama like me with littles who wake you up before it is humanly acceptable to be awake, never fear. I've got the solution, and it is possible to do what the greats do. Drumroll, please ...

I create a nighttime routine. Brilliant, right?

I worked with the reality I had. Having this routine helps me feel in control of the day ahead just like a morning routine does. The only difference is after doing my routine, I get in a solid restful night's sleep. And really, isn't that even better?

You'll wake up feeling more calm and less hurried so you can start your day on the right foot.

*Claim the life you want!*

## *Help is not coming*

Most of us don't understand that we are in control. If you're waiting for somebody to come and save you from whatever challenge is in front of you, I'm so sorry to have to be the one to tell you this... but help is not coming from the outside.

Help is not on the way; it's already here. It is who you are on the inside. And yes, you are strong. Don't let that voice in the back of your head screw you. You have fought too hard, done too much, worked too hard, and given up too much to let it all go.

*Affirmation:*
*Throw anything at me. I've got this.*

## *Make a NOT-TO-DO list*

This would include things you know are not serving you, things you get sucked into, and things you are ultimately trying to avoid.

Taking a glance at your not-to-do list in the morning can be a great way to stay on track to have the kind of day, and ultimately the kind of life, that you are striving towards.

*Get great at what you are already good at and delegate the rest.*

## *Choose your own adventure*

How do you see yourself? How do you want others to see you?

We all want clarity in our lives and a clear understanding of who we are as individuals, where we fit into the social network, and where life is taking us.

Your vision will be the guiding arrow in helping you achieve this clarity and keeping you on your path.

What is your story? You are, after all, the only one who can write it.

*Affirmation:*
*Life is happening for me, not to me.*

## *Do it all wrong on your way to doing it all right*

When you are working on something new, you're gonna suck at first. No one was awesome at something the first time they tried. The secret to sticking with a new skill is to be okay with not being perfect, and to make small progress every day.

Start small and build a solid foundation to grow from. Once you get past the initial pain of the learning curve, you will surpass even your own expectations!

Oak trees start from acorns—don't be afraid to start small. If you just keep moving forward, you are going to get there.

> “ *Discipline weighs ounces while regret weighs tons.* ”
>
> *JIM ROHN*

## *You don't need to figure it out alone*

Put yourself in community with others who can help you figure it out. Save yourself some grief and learn from someone who has already been there.

Find a mentor, a teacher, or even an author who has done what you want to do, been where you want to go, or has the life you want to have. Learn from them. They will share the mistakes they made so you don't have to. Their job is to collapse time for you so you can achieve your dreams faster.

*Community over competition: a rising tide lifts all ships.*

## *For things to change, you need to change*

The strongest need of a human being is to stay consistent with how they identify themselves. This makes it so hard to change! The truth is that for things to change for you, you must change.

Take ownership of your life and start small. Make one small change today, and you're already on the path to a new you.

Success comes from taking constant action and learning from each failure.

*Ask yourself: What can I take action on right now?*

## *Your environment is stronger than your willpower*

Make sure you are setting yourself up for success in your life, and for what you want your life to look like.

If you want to exercise more, then put your running shoes in the front hall so you see them each morning as you head to work. Keep your gym bag and a full bottle of water in the car. Choose a gym that is on the way to work.

Make it easy for you to say yes to the things you want in your life. If you want to get better at playing guitar, don't keep it in the case in the closet; bring it out to the living room and put it on a stand. Make sure it stays tuned.

The way in which you set up your environment matters and plays a big part in determining whether you stick to your life goals.

> "*It is better to be ready and not to go, then to go and not be ready.*"
>
> UNKNOWN

## *Lean into fear*

Fear is fuel. Fear is the threshold of limitation.

It's good that you are uncomfortable when you try something new. It's taking action that kicks fear to the curb. If you are not uncomfortable, you're not growing. Fear is the threshold for the next level of life. Lean in.

*When you start to spin out of control, focus on what you can control, not what you are afraid of.*

## *Allow your dream to lead*

You want to feel alive again. You were called to do more.

If other people don't understand, that is okay! It's not their dream, after all. It's yours.

Claim it. Follow it. Live it.

*Affirmation:*
*I am meant for more.*

# The Tyranny of How

Don't get stuck in the "tyranny of how" you are going to achieve your goal, as Tony Robbins teaches. Get out of your own way and take bold, uncomfortable action.

The why comes first. The how comes later.

Reasons come first; answers come second.

Decide on the WHY, and the HOW will come with action.

You just need to know the next right step. You don't need to see the entire path.

> *"Never place a period where God has placed a comma."*
>
> GRACIE ALLEN

# Closing Thoughts

I will leave you with just this one thought: Be you.

Find what makes you happy and run with it. Run with reckless abandon and don't worry about the stones and curves on your road. They will still be there, but hopefully after reading this guide you are able to find a few ways to overcome the obstacles which will undoubtedly arise and continue with your smooth ride.

Some of the things in this book might work for you and some of them might not ring true. That is exactly the point! We are all different and each one of us will draw something different from the words in this book. We might even interpret the same idea in different ways.

My hope is simply that you can take something away from this read, whether it be a better understanding of yourself or someone else in your life or how to handle stress. Maybe you got inspired or found peace.

Each of us is different but I am confident that everyone can take something from these collective suggestions to make a change for the better in their lives or in the lives of someone around them. And that really is the purpose for me.

# *Inspiration and Mentors*

I want to be fully transparent and acknowledge that none of these ideas, practices, tips, tricks, habits, quotes, affirmations, etc., are mine. The credit goes to the many teachers and mentors along the way who have inspired me. I have learned from many, too many to recall, but here is a list of some of the inspiring leaders and teachers who have inspired me and in doing that, have co-created this book for you.

Brendon Burchard, Brian Tracy, David Chilton, Dr. David R. Hamilton, Dean Graziosi, Don Miguel Ruiz, Elizabeth Gilbert, Esther Hicks, Evy Coupe, Gala Darling, Gay Hendricks, Glennon Doyle, Gretchen Rubin, James Clear, Jamie Glowacki, Jamie Kern Lima, Jenna Kutcher, Kimberly Lucas, Krista Ripma, Lisa Bilyeu, Lisa Nichols, Megan Sumrell, Mel Robbins, Mellissa Seaman, Michael Newton, Pema Chödrön, Rachel Hollis, Reese Evans, Rhonda Byrne, Rob Dial, Roxie Nafousi, Sarah Knight, Shakti Gawain, Sheryl Sandberg, Stephen Covey, Teal Swan, Tony Robbins, and Dr. Wayne W. Dyer.

# Thank you for reading my book!

If you are interested in hiring me to speak at a workshop, conference, event, or meeting please be in touch at info@jillwright.ca.

Did you love this book?

**Please consider taking two minutes right now to leave a helpful review on Amazon letting me know what you thought of the book.**

I really appreciate your honest feedback and I love hearing what you thought about the book! Your input can help make the next version of this book, and my future books even better.

A review goes a LONG way in helping get this book into more people's hands.

Thank you so much!!

Jill

JILL WRIGHT IS A THIRTY-SOMETHING MAMA OF TWO LIVING IN OTTAWA, CANADA. SHE IS THE HOST OF THE GROW LIKE A MOTHER PODCAST AND IS A MOTIVATIONAL SPEAKER. SHE LOVES READING, MOUNTAINS, THE OUTDOORS AND ANYTHING PERSONAL DEVELOPMENT.